The North–South Dialogue

Studies in International Political Economy will present new work, from a multinational stable of authors, on major issues, theoretical and practical, in the international political economy.

General Editor

Susan Strange, Professor of International Relations,
London School of Economics and Political Science, England

Consulting Editors

Ladd Hollist, Visiting Associate Professor,
Brigham Young University, USA

Karl Kaiser, Director, Research Institute of the German Society
for Foreign Affairs, Bonn, and Professor of Political Science,
University of Cologne, West Germany

William Leohr, Graduate School of International Studies,
University of Denver, USA

Joseph Nye, Professor of Government, Harvard University, USA

Already Published

The Political Economy of New and Old Industrial Countries
The East European Economies in the 1970s
Defence, Technology and International Integration
Japan and Western Europe
Tax Havens and Offshore Finance

Forthcoming Titles

International Political Economy—A Text
Dependency Transformed
International Regimes for the Control of Nuclear Technology

The North–South Dialogue

A Brief History

Charles A. Jones

Frances Pinter (Publishers), London

© Charles A. Jones 1983

First Published in Great Britain in 1983 by
Frances Pinter (Publishers) Limited
5 Dryden Street, London WC2E 9NW

British Library Cataloguing in Publication Data

Jones, Charles A.
   The north–south dialogue.
   1. Economic development   2. Inequalities
   I. Title
   330.9   HD82
   ISBN 0–86187–258–4

Typeset by Joshua Associates, Oxford
Printed by SRP Ltd., Exeter

For
Linda
and
Kate

CONTENTS

PREFACE

My intention has been to provide a short narrative of the dialogue between rich and poor states in international organizations during the eventful decade which began in 1973. In telling this story I have tried to hint at the ideological disputes, political conflicts, historical antecedents, and economic technicalities which make the dialogue so intriguing to a wide range of specialists in the social sciences, to indicate the multiplicity of forums in which the single dialogue has been pursued, and to do so without ever losing touch with the central chronological line.

That the book came to be written at all was because, when talking with undergraduates reading economics, I often observed how difficult it was for them to place recent debates between economists in their institutional context and so recognize and discount the ideological and polemical content of the avowedly technical papers they were directed to read. In consequence they often appeared to be getting very much less pleasure out of the discipline than they might, which seemed a shame.

Looking for a work to recommend to such students I found many excellent papers and rather fewer full-length works on the recent period. Naturally, however, there was a considerable lag between the occurrence of important events and their treatment in academic periodicals, and still more, in scholarly monographs. There were also few if any general works, most being concerned with a single forum, and the stress was almost always on political or economic rather than historical analysis, a point which struck me most forcibly. I felt confident that if I were to rely entirely on secondary works and conclude with a chapter based principally on the daily press, I could produce an analytical narrative which saw the dialogue safely round the corner it began to turn in 1978 and on to a new course. It would be a first approximation, and experience suggested that the result might be condemned for a somewhat eccentric and hybrid methodology, but this seemed a small price to pay for a text which, at least for a year or two, might be better able than most to give readers new to the subject a feeling for how current events linked up with the recent past.

I have not weighed the book down with any discussion of terms. It is assumed that the reader has a rough understanding of what sorts of nations consider themselves to belong to a Third World distinct from the relatively rich states of North America, Western

Europe, and Australasia on the one hand, and the centrally-planned economies of the Soviet bloc on the other. I have taken the Third World, the South, and the Group of 77 to denote sets of states which overlap so closely that the terms may generally be used as synonyms. I have not bothered unduly about allotting marginal cases such as South Africa, Israel, Portugal, Spain, Yugoslavia, Argentina, and the like.

I have followed the convention of employing abbreviations and acronyms freely even though I know that many readers find it either offensive or confusing. To the former I can only reply that the convention exists, and that part of the duty of the author of an introduction must be to familiarize readers with just such quirks as this in the more specialist literature. To the latter I would point out the table of abbreviations which follows this preface and is intended to serve the same sort of purpose as those long lists of characters and their relationships which are generally to be found at the start of English translations of the Russian classics. I can only hope that it will enlighten more than it deters, and add that in the text I have tried to mention institutions by their full titles more than once before resorting to the abbreviation and to use the full title again when returning to them after a lapse of more than a few pages.

It remains to thank my wife, Linda, for her help, which was appreciated all the more since the book was written at a time when her own career and our growing family were making strong demands on her. It was my post at the University of Warwick which first led me to take an interest in North–South relations and a period of sabbatical leave which provided the respite from teaching duties which allowed me to write the book. My thanks go also, therefore, to the University and to those of my colleagues who have kindly taken over the mercifully light administrative tasks I normally perform or who have otherwise helped with the book. My particular thanks go to Joy Gardner, Barry Buzan, and Gowher Rizvi.

ABBREVIATIONS

ACP	African Caribbean and Pacific
ANCOM	Andean Common Market
ANRPC	Association of Natural Rubber Producing Countries
ASEAN	Association of South-East Asian Nations
CAP	Common Agricultural Policy (of the EEC)
CFF	(IMF) Compensatory Finance Facility
CIEC	Conference on International Economic Co-operation
CIPEC	Conseil Intergouvernemental des Pays Exportateurs de Cuivre (Intergovernmental Council of Copper Exporting Countries)
COMECON	Council for Mutual Economic Assistance
CTC	(UN) Centre on Transnational Corporations
CTN	(UN) Commission on Transnational Corporations
CVD	Countervailing Duty
DC	Developed Country
DFI	Direct Foreign Investment
ECLA	(UN) Economic Commission for Latin America
ECOSOC	(UN) Economic and Social Council
EEC	European Economic Community
EEZ	Exclusive Economic Zone
EUA	European Unit of Account
FAO	(UN) Food and Agriculture Organization
FNLA	Frente Nacionale de Libertação de Angola (National Front for the Liberation of Angola)
GAB	General Agreement to Borrow
GATT	General Agreement on Tariffs and Trade
GNP	Gross National Product
GSP	General (or Generalized) System(s) of Preference
IAEA	International Atomic Energy Authority
IBA	International Bauxite Association
IBRD	International Bank for Reconstruction and Development
ICA	Individual Commodity Agreement
ICA	International Coffee Agreement
ICNT	Informal Composite Negotiating Text
IDA	International Development Association
ILC	(UN) International Law Commission
ILO	International Labour Office
IMF	International Monetary Fund

INRA	International Natural Rubber Agreement
IPC	Integrated Programme for Commodities
IRB	International Resources Bank
IRC	(UN) Information and Research Centre (on TNCs)
ISA	International Seabed Authority
ISA	International Sugar Agreement
ISI	Import Substituting Industrialization
ITA	International Tin Agreement
ITO	International Tin Organization
LAFTA	Latin American Free Trade Area
LAIA	Latin American Integration Association
LDC	Less Developed Country
LLGDS	Land-Locked and Geographically Disadvantaged States
LTA	Long-Term Arrangement (regarding Cotton Textiles)
MFA	Multifibre Arrangement
MNC	Multinational Corporation
MNE	Multinational Enterprise
MPLA	Popular Movement for the Liberation of Angola
MTN	(GATT) Multilateral Trade Negotiations
NAFINSA	Nacional Financiera (Mexico)
NAM	Non-Aligned Movement
NIC	Newly Industrializing Country
NIEO	New International Economic Order
NPT	Nuclear Proliferation Treaty
NSG	Nuclear Suppliers' Group
NTB	Non-Tariff Barrier
OAPEC	Organization of Arab Petroleum Exporting Countries
OAU	Organization of African Unity
OECD	Organization for Economic Co-operation and Development
OPEC	Organization of Petroleum Exporting Countries
ORS	Open Register System
PLO	Palestine Liberation Organization
RTA	Reciprocal Trade Agreements (Act)
SALT	Strategic Arms Limitation Talks/Treaty
SDR	Special Drawing Right
STABEX	Stabilization of Exports (EEC/ACP)
SUNFED	Special United Nations Fund for Economic Development
TNC	Transnational Corporation
TNE	Transnational Enterprise
UN	United Nations
UNCLOS	United Nations Conference on the Law of the Sea

UNCSTD	United Nations Conference on Science and Technology for Development
UNCTAD	United Nations Conference on Trade and Development
UNCTC	United Nations Centre on Transnational Corporations
UNCTCDC	United Nations Conference on Technical Co-operation between Developing Countries
UNIDO	United Nations Industrial Development Organization
UNITA	National Union for the Total Independence of Angola
WIPO	World Intellectual Property Organization

1 THE THIRD WORLD ADOPTS A COLLECTIVE STRATEGY

'North–South Dialogue' is very much a phrase of the 1970s. Arab oil-power and American humiliation in South–East Asia combined to direct the attention of western politicians, journalists, and publics increasingly toward the interminable succession of technically complex international negotiations on trade, money, and a host of lesser issues, in which it appeared that a new balance of power was to be struck between the industrialized West and the successor states of the old European empires in Africa, Asia, and Latin America. Satisfactory outcomes in these negotiations were regarded by third-world states as essential to healthy economic and political development because it was widely assumed that the prevailing structure of international institutions served the narrow interests of powerful industrialized states at the expense of the poorer countries of the South.

There are therefore two key sets of questions to be faced before addressing the events of the 1970s directly. First of all, why did so many third-world states think it politic to adopt a strategy of collective peaceful confrontation with the West in international negotiations as a leading element in their foreign policies from the 1960s. Why was this strategy adopted just when it was? Why was it thought likely to prove effective? Why was it preferred to alternative available strategies? Second, what was the condition of the various international organizations which were to provide the stage for North–South debate on the eve of the conflict? What made third-world leaders think that they might be able to work effectively through an institutional structure which they believed to be biased against them from the start and which it was their intention to transform?

The first two chapters of this book attempt to answer these questions. In the remainder of this chapter the origins of the collective strategy are explored. Some account is given of the way in which the United States and Britain encouraged the growth of assumptions about material progress and industrialization in third-world countries during the Second World War but subsequently frustrated any expectations they might have aroused as they became enmeshed in the logic of the Cold War and the political quagmire of decolonization. The very different world view of the Latin American nations is traced. Then the variety of strategies open to independent third-world states in the post-war world and the limitations of these strategies are surveyed before the evolution of an ideology and a set of practical circumstances supporting the adoption of a strategy of collective negotiation in international forums is finally examined.

The Second World War

The effects of the Second World War on the colonial territories and independent states of Africa, Asia, and Latin America were profound and diverse. For some the war offered great economic opportunities. The belligerents were large-scale buyers of food and raw materials at prices above the low levels reached by many commodities between the wars. By devoting their industrial capacity to war production and rationing shipping space severely, the belligerents encouraged import-substituting manufacturing industry in their former export markets. At the same time, however, they undoubtedly hampered the growth of new industrial economies by their inability or unwillingness to provide the inputs of capital, technical expertise, and machinery which would have been available in peacetime and by the sheer strength of the countervailing demand they exerted for traditional unprocessed exports. Non-belligerents far from the theatres of war, in Latin America especially, found it frustrating to see the proceeds of their vast sales of raw materials to Britain piling up in the form of sterling balances in London which could neither be converted to United States dollars nor used to buy British machinery and sophisticated manufactured goods to assist further industrialization at home.

The Latin American states were at least spared the pain and indignity of invasion and occupation and the social dislocation of extensive military mobilization. In the Old World the experience of colonial troops, some of them fighting on European soil, widened horizons and destroyed illusions of European superiority and invulnerability. Early Axis victories in Europe and Asia, especially the ignominious defeat of France in 1940 and the spectacular victories of the Japanese early in 1942, provided further evidence of the weakness of the colonial powers. More than this it put the British and the Free French in a weak position when negotiating with their colonial subjects for political support during the remainder of the war. Promises of greater autonomy had to be made to local groups in those territories where military control was retained, though concession coexisted uneasily with repression of those leaders and organizations whose nationalism had about it the least breath of disloyalty or subversion. In South-East Asia it remained to be seen whether European political authority could ever be re-established in territories where the always perilous legitimacy of the imperial regimes had been shattered by military defeat and the Japanese had been able to project themselves, not entirely unreasonably, as liberators. Elsewhere the nominal independence of states such as Iran, Egypt, Libya, and Thailand was trampled on as the belligerents single-mindedly pursued their strategic objectives.

It was certainly not until 1943 that any clear sense of the significance of this diversity of experience or the tendency of great power policy towards the lesser powers and the colonial empires became apparent. How could it when the eventual outcome of the war was still undecided and the chief participants had still to settle firmly on their post-war international economic policies? But from the middle of 1942 it became apparent that a combination of the administratively ingenious British rationing and industrial mobilization systems and the sheer scale of United States shipbuilding programmes had defeated the German strategy of isolating Britain within a U-boat cordon. In the East, United States victories over Japan near Midway and on Guadalcanal Island in mid-1942 were followed early the following year by the powerful psychological blow of German defeat at Stalingrad. So 1943 became the year in which policy-makers at the highest levels in the United States and Britain, now confident of ultimate victory, paused to examine and unravel the skein of preparations for the post-war era which their officials had woven for them.

It happened that the external economic policy of leading figures in the United States administration at this time was liberal almost to the point of Utopianism. In so far as it was to affect the poorer independent countries of the world, this policy had two chief strands. The first was a commitment to encourage economic development by means of rapid industrialization, in the belief that the loss of exports of traditional products from the United States would be more than compensated for by remitted profits from subsidiaries of United States firms engaged in local manufacture of those same products in Latin America, together with the enlarged exports of United States capital goods and new kinds of consumer goods which would result as Latin America developed larger firms and better paid industrial workforces and adopted North American patterns of life. This view of the future appears to have been accepted by the United States administration from the mid-1930s and was soon after acquiesced in by the British. A senior official at the British Board of Trade, voicing what he termed 'our general view' early in 1942, argued that 'collaboration with the South American States in their natural development will help our own industries best in the long run' and that 'our own best hope . . . may be to develop the more modern industries and abandon those that can no longer compete'.[1]

But was this official encouragement of peripheral industrialization to be envisaged within autarkic trading blocs or economic empires, each dominated by one or other of the great powers, or was it, by contrast, to be achieved within an open world economy in which multilateral systems of trade and payments allowed a full play to the principle of division of labour in accordance with comparative advantage? Much of the evidence of the 1930s pointed to the first of these two alternatives. Britain had adopted many of the same nationalistic economic techniques as Germany and Italy: exchange controls, higher tariffs and quantitative controls on trade, and, in 1932, imperial preference. The United States too had imposed serious barriers to international trade and triggered similar actions from other trading nations by raising its tariff in 1930. Although the USA had begun to reverse this nationalistic policy under the Reciprocal Trade Agreements Act of 1934, powerful protectionist opposition persisted at very high levels of the bureaucracy and the legislature to this, as to so many of the policies of the Roosevelt administration, so that as late as the early 1940s there was still a lobby with support within the State Department pushing the idea of a formal system of western-hemisphere trading preferences that would bind Latin America to its powerful neighbours and bring about a marked diminution in the formerly strong economic positions held by Britain and Germany in many of the republics.

If it is clear retrospectively that the USA was firmly set upon a liberal course after 1934, it was less clear to her allies at the time. Import duties collected, which had amounted to 51 per cent of the value of dutiable imports in the first half of the decade, fell to 39 per cent during the later 1930s, and there was a substantial increase in United States trade during the four years after the RTA Act passed Congress. However, although the RTA Act was multilateralist in intent and stipulated that each bilateral trade agreement negotiated under it should include an unconditional most-favoured-nation clause extending any particular concessions made to *all* trading partners of the USA, the practical effect by the end of the decade had been to extend US trade with countries with which agreements had been concluded very much faster than total trade. US exports to trade-agreement states rose by 63 per cent in the period 1934/5–1938/9, and imports from them by 22 per cent. In the meantime exports to and imports from states with which the US had no such agreements rose by only 32 and 16 per cent respectively. Moreover many of the trade agreements concluded before 1939 were with other American states including Canada, Brazil, Cuba, Haiti, Colombia, Guatemala, and Nicaragua, and to this extent the policy was consistent in practice, though not in theory, with a hemispheric approach to international trade. The sorts of concessions yielded by the US in negotiations with other American states were likely to be of more use to the remaining non-agreement Latin American states than to industrialized countries such as Britain or Germany, which had a quite different spectrum of exports. Agreements with Belgium in 1935 and France and the Netherlands the following year may have helped redress the balance. Yet as late as 1960 over 400 industrial products still faced high US rates of duty dating back to 1930.[2]

By 1943 most remaining doubts about the ambiguous tendency of US commercial policy had been quelled, and even the British, who harboured deep suspicions of American intentions south of the Rio Grande, were persuaded that Secretary of State Cordell Hull and multilateralism had won the day.[3] Thereafter it became possible for the Allies to depict the war not simply as a struggle between Fascism and representative democracy, but as a contest between what now became identified as the Axis concept of tightly controlled autarkic economic empires and their own more liberal idea of an open world economy.

This simple if less than totally honest dichotomy became the foundation stone of an Anglo-American liberal historiography, which was to influence attitudes toward the North–South dialogue thirty years later quite directly. The story would go like this. Economic nationalism and restrictionism in the period between the two world wars, initiated by Germany and its future allies and indulged in by Britain and the United States only with the greatest reluctance, were to be regarded as a major cause of the 1939–45 conflict; indirectly, because they had caused dislocation, unemployment, and political turmoil in Germany and Japan; directly, because the expanding web of restrictions in the 1930s had been unashamedly used as a means of aggrandizement and tool of foreign policy by Germany, especially in Eastern Europe.[4] The system of managed liberalism set up by the Allies in the mid-1940s under United States leadership was to be regarded, therefore, as an essential peacekeeping system and a democratic response to fascism. Precisely because it was underwritten and supported in a way that permitted the relatively free operation of market forces, the international economic order underpinned by the Bretton Woods institutions and the General Agreement on Tariffs and Trade exhibited a most remarkable tendency towards increased international trade and unprecedentedly rapid growth in participant states, and nowhere was the rate of growth of income per capita faster than in those economies in Latin America, Asia, and the Middle East which were experiencing rapid industrialization. To challenge the post-war order was therefore to risk a collapse of the prosperity of the 1950s and 1960s and a recurrence of the poverty, under-utilization of resources, and international aggression of the 1930s.

In this schema, economic liberalism could be viewed not only as a force for peace through prosperity, but also, by North Americans, as a democratic and anti-imperialist policy expressive of the strain of radicalism which many believed to have been central to the liberation struggle and early years of their own state. Americans were inclined to regard European overseas empires and the statist attitude to economic management typical of the continental European powers as obstructive anachronisms and to be irritated by the constraints they had often placed on burgeoning United States enterprise. To be sure, the North Americans had a record of imperialism themselves in Mexico, the Caribbean, and the Pacific, but they found it possible to rationalize this as being in large measure the outcome of a progressive war against the corrupt and creaking Spanish Empire at the turn of the century. It is undoubtedly anachronistic, but it is not entirely inaccurate, to suggest that liberal North Americans had in the backs of their minds a notion of themselves as leaders of the Third World against European imperialism. So they were all the more put out to find themselves increasingly cast as imperialists-in-chief in the post-war world.

The prevailing view by the mid-1940s, then, as much in London as in Washington, was that in what we now call the Third World, just as in war-torn Europe, economic liberalism was the key to future prosperity, and prosperity the means to civil order and good international relations. The system of international economic institutions, the new international economic order of the 1940s, which was later to be so intensely resented by third-world politicians and represented as imperialist in effect, was originally conceived of as progressive and anti-imperialist; unless this is understood the extreme irritation and hostility of United States establishment liberals faced with what they perceive as uninformed and wrong-headed allegations about the motives of their predecessors and perniciously destructive proposals for reform can hardly be understood.

*Economic Nationalist and Anti-colonialist Perceptions
in the Third World*

Many Latin Americans, then as now, would have found this version
of events ludicrous and unrecognizable. Minds formed by the experience of the 1930s could not look forward to a post-war liberal
economic order with much confidence. Disastrous falls in commodity prices against a background of disillusion with representative
democracy had brought Getulio Vargas to power in Brazil by a
bloodless coup in 1930. The same year of economic crisis saw the
democratically elected President of Argentina deposed by the
military. In many other lesser republics the slump has contributed
very directly to constitutional breakdown. These events produced
an understandable reaction against economic specialization.

Low commodity prices and the collapse of international capital
markets necessarily had considerable influence on capacity to import,
and made the adoption of strategies of import-substituting industrialization almost inevitable. But this policy went further in
Argentina than in, say, Australia, at least partly because it coincided
with military thinking, however spurious, on the strategic value of
self-sufficiency, which was much more strongly represented in post-
coup Argentina than in democratic Australia.[5] In some, though by
no means all, Latin American republics this acquiescence in autarky
was accompanied by overt sympathy for the Axis powers. Even
where this was not the case, nationalist attacks on foreign-owned
public utilities and extractive ventures damaged relations with
Britain, the United States, and other parent states, and these were
further strained by the exclusive tendencies of the commercial
policies of the great powers themselves in the 1930s and by their
subsidies to domestic agriculture. Argentina, for example, was a
major casualty of the system of imperial preferences introduced by
Britain and her dominions in 1932.

The message seemed clear. Britain and the other great powers
were fair-weather liberals. When their vital economic interests were
threatened they unhesitatingly resorted to massive state intervention,
as much in the external as in the domestic sphere, so insulating themselves wherever possible from the worst effects of a slump for which
they themselves were primarily responsible. Latin Americans suffered
disproportionately, partly because their state apparatuses were less
strong, efficient, and responsive than those of the great powers,
partly because of the peculiar economic characteristics of demand
for primary commodities, and partly because of differences in the

level of organization and bargaining power of their firms and workers relative to those of the industrialized powers.

These cynical suspicions of the sincerity and universality of the new liberalism soon received confirmation. After the failure of a premature attempt to restore the convertibility of sterling in 1947, forced on a reluctant British Government by the United States, it was not in fact until the end of the 1950s that the major European currencies became convertible. The Havana Charter for a new International Trade Organization under United Nations auspices, which incorporated a number of concessions to primary producers, became a dead letter after the strong protectionist lobby in the United States Congress prevented ratification in 1950. At the same time, growing fear of the Soviet Union was to make the United States hostile towards modernizing regimes elsewhere, which it rightly or wrongly felt to be tainted with Communism, and much more tolerant than it might otherwise have been of the resurgent mercantilism and lingering imperialism of the Europeans. The strategic value of these and other allies on the flanks of the Communist bloc was constantly to distort and compromise the original ideological purity of United States universal liberalism, effectively overcoming official opposition to the trade preferences extended by the European Economic Community (EEC) to the third-world former dependencies of its members in defiance of the GATT, the highly protectionist Common Agricultural Policy (CAP) of the EEC, the continuing protectionism of an increasingly wealthy Japan, and the evidently repressive and illiberal character of client states such as South Vietnam, Iran or Pakistan.[6] There would be periodic attempts to recover moral integrity —the well-meaning but short-sighted and disruptive Nixon offensive against the production of narcotics in 1971 was one, and the Carter human rights policy another—but these bursts of idealism were seldom considered, always short-lived, and generally served simply to muddy the waters.[7]

If there was dissatisfaction in Latin America with the emerging realities of post-war United States foreign policy, there was a corresponding dissatisfaction in Africa and Asia with the continued presence there of European colonial regimes. Peoples whose experience of European rule scarcely antedated the slide into mercantilism at the end of the nineteenth century could hardly be expected to share United States enthusiasm for the benefits that had allegedly stemmed from free trade under a *pax britannica* before 1914 and might now be resuscitated under a new *pax americana*. In India, under British rule throughout the so-called liberal interlude, the last days of the old mercantilism linked up by way of philanthropic utilitarianism and strategic railways with the revived mercantilism of the late-nineteenth century; the seam hardly showed.

The first concern of these states was political independence. This was conceded throughout much of South and South-East Asia during the first post-war decade and to many African and some Caribbean territories by the mid-1960s, though the speed of withdrawal should not conceal the extreme reluctance with which Europeans sometimes departed or the violence of the independence struggle in territories such as Algeria, Vietnam, Malaya, and Kenya. But once independent, the new states very soon encountered the limits which had been imposed on their freedom of action by decades of mercantilist management. Many were very poor indeed, dependent for foreign-exchange earnings on exports of a handful of cash crops or mineral ores, products often originally developed by the colonial regimes for revenue purposes and sold largely in the metropolitan markets of the former imperial nations. Few had experienced substantial industrial development. The first generation of leaders, after riding to power on a wave of millenarian support, found themselves, within a very few years, face to face with massive discontent and seemingly powerless to act upon its source, deep in the complex and mercurial capitalist world economy.

Policy Options in the Post-war World

What then were the choices facing third-world policy-makers in the 1950s and 1960s? For the smallest and weakest states, including many newly independent African territories, there seemed little option but to hold tight to the apron strings of a major power. Many continued to look to France or Britain for financial and technical assistance, higher education, and markets in what was clearly a quasi-colonial relationship. Others, sometimes on ideological grounds, changed one patron for another. When the United States stopped buying Cuban sugar the Soviet Union stood ready to step into its place. Other Caribbean states began to move closer to the United States following independence, less for ideological than for practical reasons.

Because of the relative openness of the new international economic order, neo-colonial dependence of this sort could be tempered by diversification. Algeria, Tanzania, Egypt, India, and Yugoslavia spring to mind as states whose governments were able at various periods to extract negotiating advantage from East–West rivalries, so spreading and consequently reducing their dependence. Often this strategy was accompanied by much fine talk about economic independence, or to use the felicitous phrase of the Tanzanian leader, Julius Nyerere, of self-reliance. But generally it was only the larger third-world economies, India, Indonesia, and the major Latin American republics, that were able to go very far in the direction of truly autarkic development, and even they encountered heavy costs which were becoming unacceptable by the 1960s. In the first place, even the largest third-world states often exerted insufficient demand to allow local industrial firms to achieve fully the economies of scale in production offered by the best available technology. A common pattern, examplified in the Argentine motor industry of the 1960s, was for the typically high tariff wall to protect a surprisingly large number of sub-optimal plants, some owned by local private investors or the state, others by multinational corporations based in the United States or Europe, and all operating substantially below capacity. The multinationals were there because the logic of oligopolistic competition suggested that 'follow the leader' was the safest rule. It could be disastrous in the long run for the others to let small markets with high rates of growth be cornered by any single competing firm, lest high profits yielded by that peripheral market five or ten years later might be fed back into the more sluggish United States or European home markets and used there as a lever to increase market share. In the meantime, with careful attention to costs and by the fullest exercise of the administrative and financial advantages which they possessed over local firms, the multinationals might hope to break even or make a modest profit to remit to head office. A substantial proportion of the profits in the protected industry were therefore often taken out of the economy, so that much of the intended dynamic effect of the policy was lost. In addition there were constraints on reducing unit costs by expanding export sales. Having opted out of post-war international trade liberalization and with very small shares of total world trade, these countries had little negotiating strength when bargaining for improved access to the rich industrial economies of the United States and Europe. They could seek export markets locally, of course, but this strategy, considered a little later, was no panacea. And aside from official constraints on exports in the form of tariffs and quotas, there were private constraints. Third-world subsidiaries of large multinationals were sometimes forbidden by head office from exporting in competition with other firms within the group.

The favourable balance of payments effects expected from import substituting industrialization also had a tendency to slip away. The very high effective rates of protection accorded to favoured industries were ultimately expressed in high prices to the consumer. This had several effects. It kept demand low and hence contributed to the high unit costs of the industries concerned, but it also affected those sectors of the economy which were virtually obliged to use the products of local high-cost industries as inputs. In many countries agriculture met a large part of the cost of protectionism in the shape of scarce or expensive farm machinery and fertilizers. Agriculture was also affected by the drain of labour to the cities, attracted by the prospect of relatively highly-paid jobs in manufacturing industry, and frequently suffered from overvalued exchange rates, an index of the success of government control over imports, but one which discouraged traditional exports of raw materials. This negative protection or discrimination against agriculture frequently resulted in declining local production of foodstuffs and growing net imports of cheaper farm products from overseas, wiping out some of the foreign-exchange earnings accruing from imports of machinery and fertilizers forgone and counteracting the fundamental objective of the ISI strategy, which had been to liberate foreign exchange earnings for the service of debts and the purchase of capital goods needed for further industrialization.

Then there were further problems arising from the role of multinational corporations. To begin with these firms frequently earned and remitted what were, in part, monopoly rents arising from the state policy of protection rather than economic profits arising from cost competition. In effect they were reaping the benefit of policies designed to help develop national bourgeoisies, and they were doing so at the expense of other local sectors. In addition they often contributed to balance of payments crises as the volume of inward capital flow arising from new projects together with exports by the multinationals gradually came to be exceeded by the outward flow of remittances to cover royalties, profits, and imports of components and equipment. India provides a good example of just such a balance of payments squeeze. Foreign-exchange reserves fell rapidly during the 1950s. To fill the gap the Indian government became increasingly reliant on aid from the developed West. But western agencies demanded changes in policy as a condition of assistance, and in 1957 the government relaxed the constraints it had placed on foreign-owned firms since independence ten years before. This was in any case expedient, since to open up new opportunities for DFI in India was to encourage existing firms to reinvest rather than remit profits overseas, and this helped the balance of payments in the short term. Liberalization contributed to a fifteen-year phase of steadily reducing trade deficits as ISI began to reduce imports. But these were increasingly offset by a deteriorating invisible balance as multinationals grew larger and remitted larger amounts, until the Janata government felt bound to tighten up the Indian DFI regime again in the mid-1970s.[8]

By the 1960s, countries which had followed autarkic economic policies for the past two or three decades were hard up against the kinds of difficulties that have been described here. Moreover the root causes of these problems were widely exposed in a number of lucid analyses of the limits of ISI published during the sixties and early seventies.[9] The more powerful third-world states were searching for new economic policies that might provide a way round the impasse.

It will be as well to dismiss briefly one logically obvious but practically irrelevant category of solution. National economy-building by conquest and annexation had served well enough in Europe and North America, but Europe and North America were unwilling to see it adopted elsewhere. There were considerable opportunities in post-colonial Africa and Asia for the rationalization of ludicrous boundaries imposed by Europe and the consequent strengthening of some states and economies by wars of aggression or secession. Few of these opportunities have been taken, however, and at least part of the reason for this has been that regional power politics have constantly been overshadowed by East–West rivalries. The superpowers have generally preferred to endorse stability even at the price of corruption or stagnation within their spheres of influence. In areas of confrontation between East and West—the Middle East, the Caribbean, and South-East Asia—the risk of sparking off a more general war has generally led patrons to restrain their clients, preferring lingering wars of attrition coupled with diplomacy to more sweeping Napoleonic solutions. It is not immediately evident that this policy of centrally ordered *bellum interruptum* has been more humane or conducive to welfare than a more anarchic system would have been.

If the effective use of force was largely ruled out by great power disapproval, it was quite the reverse with peaceful economic integration. United States governments were well-disposed to attempts to speed development by the creation of free-trade areas or common markets, and GATT rules which would otherwise have outlawed these preferential arrangements made specific exception for them. Moreover by the 1960s that curious blend of idealism and mercantilism, the EEC, was under way, providing—or so it seemed to many observers—living proof of the efficacy of regional co-operation.

Regional integration has been a facet of third-world economic policy ever since the late 1950s. There have been numerous experiments.

The Latin American Free Trade Area (LAFTA), established in 1959, brought together eleven republics in an ambitious attempt to liberalize intra-regional trade following the European model. But much of this trade was in raw materials and more than three-quarters was conducted by three of the most highly-developed member states, Argentina, Brazil, and Mexico. Besides, intra-regional trade simply was not as important to third-world states as it was to the Europeans with their highly integrated economies. On the eve of the creation of the EEC about half the foreign trade of the six founder members was mutual. For the LAFTA states the equivalent figure in 1961 was a mere six per cent of the gross product of the group. Trade liberalization appeared from the start to be of less importance to Latin America than to Europe, and of very varying value to different groups of states within LAFTA. The larger countries in the region would eventually have to gain access to developed-country markets if their more advanced industries were not to be stifled. In the meantime, the smaller members soon came to feel that the benefits of liberalization were accruing disproportionately to the major trading states and doing nothing to promote their own industrial development. Negotiations between the smaller states from 1966 led to the Cartagena Agreement of 1969 setting up an Andean Common Market (ANCOM), which placed relatively less stress on tariff reductions than LAFTA had, and much more on rational planning of industrial investment and control of direct foreign investment as a means to capture the full benefits made available by the pooling of national markets.

This move from liberal integration built around the expansion of trade and demand to a more *dirigiste* approach stressing planning investment and the supply side of the regional economy was partly a pragmatic adaptation of northern economic theory to southern realities, partly a symptom of a general drift away from the more Utopian elements in post-war liberalism that was as much evident in the inter-governmentalist tendency of the EEC by the 1970s as in the evolution of the integration movement in the Third World. Whatever its origins, the drift to statism had one important corollary. It coincided in Latin America at least with a cooling of United States support, less perhaps because of the new style of integration (though this bore heavily on North American DFI) than because the regimes which pioneered the new tendency were judged to be inimical to United States interests.[10]

Policy-makers in Washington during the fifties and sixties had been strongly influenced by the functionalist tradition, as much in their attitudes to regional integration as in their wider commitment to multilateralism. This meant, in essence, that they had seen in economic integration a political mechanism conducive to peaceful international relations. Co-operation on trade liberalization and in the management of regional development banks, transport facilities, and other institutions would forge links of friendship and understanding between official and political élites. Advancing economic integration would create bonds of material interest uniting nations. These developments would make international wars less desired, more costly, and hence less probable. At the same time, by promoting rapid economic growth they would palliate local dissent and create a climate of civil order in which it would be possible to exploit new opportunities for United States exports and investment. Now the varieties of economic nationalism favoured by Velasco in Peru and Allende in Chile, with their clear hostility to United States extractive and utility enterprises and their independent foreign policies, were simply too far from this functionalist paradigm to be viewed sympathetically by Washington.

Outside Europe and Latin America some limited experiments in regional management of specific projects were successful for a time, but more thoroughgoing integration schemes were by and large elaborate United States-backed shams. The Association of South-East Asian Nations (ASEAN) is a case in point. Though it was not and has not become a military alliance, ASEAN was clearly formed in 1967 in response to the twin threats of Vietnamese expansion and internal subversion. Malaysia, Singapore, Thailand, Indonesia, and the Philippines, even by pooling their forces, could not have matched Vietnamese strength, and they therefore felt it wiser to avoid provocation by screening their political unity behind a veneer of economic co-operation.[11] The veneer was paper thin. Exports of four of the member states to their partners expressed as a percentage of total exports in each case actually fell by between four and twelve percentage points during the decade after 1967.[12] Following the summit meeting of 1976 at Bali the moribund institution was galvanized into action. New regional institutions with a hint of supranationalism were launched. Economic policies including sectoral industrial integration were agreed. But these initiatives were clearly motivated by the withdrawal of United States forces and the unification of Vietnam, and little has happened subsequently to modify the view that ASEAN is a strategic organization first and foremost, where officials dedicated to the pursuit of economic integration will not easily be allowed to override the essentially nationalistic priorities of individual governments.

In short, regional integration has been constantly available to third-world leaders as an option promising effective enlargement of the domestic market coupled with ordered industrialization. It has never provided a complete or satisfactory solution, however, since the possibilities of and benefits from expanded intra-regional trade have generally been slight, and more *dirigiste* styles of integration, where they have been any more than window-dressing for security policies, have been beset by intra-regional national rivalries and great power suspicions.

The Adoption of a Collective Negotiating Strategy: Political and Intellectual Bases

By the 1960s autarky had been thoroughly explored as a route to sovereignty and found to be both costly and deceptive. The current world political order made the application of force to this end extremely problematic. Regional integration, though still on trial, was already being recognized as no more than a limited and imperfect vehicle. Attempts to develop a strong industrial capability and a relatively autonomous and self-sustaining pattern of economic growth by the exploitation of global market opportunities were felt to be doomed to failure because the dice were loaded in favour of the first generation of industrial economies. This dismal conjuncture favoured further experimentation, and international diplomacy appeared an especially inviting strategy for two reasons, one institutional and the other ideological.

In the first place the achievement of constitutional independence by a large number of mostly African territories after 1956 changed the complexion of the United Nations Organization. The Sudan, Morocco, and Tunisia were rapidly followed by Ghana in 1957, Guinea in 1958, and no less than eighteen former French, Belgian, Italian, and British administered territories in 1960. Total United Nations membership rose from 51 states in 1945 to 100 by 1960, and by 1979 it exceeded 150.[13] By 1963 the new states were in a position to push through amendments to the UN charter which took effect two years later. The number of elective places on the UN Security Council was increased from six to ten and membership of the Economic and Social Committee (ECOSOC) rose from eighteen to twenty-seven. While they would continue to complain of deficiencies in the UN specialized agencies, third-world states acting together could now dominate the General Assembly and use it as a forum in which to voice their grievances.[14]

At the same time that the UN became available as a platform for third-world views a new ideology was made available to unite and integrate the mass of specific complaints. The Argentine economist Raúl Prebisch, who had played an important role under the conservative military governments of the 1930s in defending the economy against world economic depression, became Executive Secretary of the United Nations Economic Commission for Latin America (ECLA) in 1949, and from this position he began to project an analysis of the world economy that turned out to have strong appeal throughout the Third World.

The central observations in the work of Prebisch concerned structural variations in the conditions of supply and demand between developed and less developed economies. In the developed world a much higher percentage of resources was devoted to manufacturing. Organized labour and oligopolistic firms were able to translate increasing demand for their products and improved productivity into higher rates of pay or bigger profit margins and to defend these gains in cyclical downturns of the world economy. To the natural barriers to entry facing any would-be producer of modern manufactured goods—the need for a distribution network, the high unit costs of small volume production, and so on—established firms and labour at the centre of the world economy were able to add a few of their own by collusion and restrictive practices. Moreover the State was willing to protect producers in sectors such as agriculture or textiles, which possessed few barriers to entry, by imposing tariffs and quantitative restrictions or granting subsidies. In short, supply was relatively inflexible in the short to medium term, partly because of administrative action and partly because resources were almost fully employed, and the result was that increased demand was expressed in higher prices for goods from the centre and accrued as rents to labour and capital.

In less-developed countries, by contrast, the opportunities for extracting economic rents were far less. The price of primary commodities, or indeed of any commodities produced in such economies, was not pulled upward by rising demand to nearly the same extent as happened in the industrialized countries. This was because the less-developed economies had substantial pools of un- or underutilized labour, and responded to increased demand by bringing this factor into play and expanding production. Similarly, their response to cyclical downturn was all too often not defensive cartelization but increased production once again, reducing prices still further in a vain attempt to maintain total earnings from a larger volume of exports.

On the demand side, too, there was a disparity. Starting from the premise that an increasing proportion of any addition to income beyond a very modest level was spent on manufactured goods, Prebisch argued that in the long run, as the general level of income increased, the rate of increase in demand for some primary products —especially foodstuffs and beverages—would fall short of the rate of increase in demand for manufactured goods.

This slack demand for primary commodities coupled with the damping effect of unutilized labour on price increases led Prebisch to expect that the price index of exports from predominantly raw material producing third-world countries would rise less rapidly than the price index of their imports, which included manufactured goods from the developed world. Economists refer to this relation as the commodity, net barter, or unit price terms of trade, and Prebisch supported his theoretical reasoning by examining the actual movement of the terms of trade in the past. He made due allowance for the fact that many highly industrialized countries such as the USA and Canada are also major exporters of primary commodities and, likewise, that some third-world countries, even by the 1950s, were exporters of manufactured goods. He also allowed for the fact that the commodity terms of trade measure relative prices without regard to volumes of imports and exports, and that third-world countries, true to form, had gone some way to meet deterioration in their commodity terms of trade by exporting larger volumes. Nevertheless he concluded that the capacity of these countries to import had been progressively eroded by the deterioration in their terms of trade, and that this had seriously inhibited their attempts to industrialize by limiting imports of capital equipment and technology. In these circumstances sensible import substituting industrializing strategies, of which Prebisch had long been an advocate, were not enough. No sooner was foreign exchange released for sophisticated imports by the local substitution of lower grade manufactures than it was effectively eaten up by increases in the prices of imports. The Third World seemed locked in a vicious circle, where their best efforts to increase the productivity of labour were simply siphoned off through the mechanism of international trade and accrued as rents to capital and labour in the rich North.[15]

This rather gloomy prognosis led Prebisch to turn against the excessive protectionism practised by many Latin American countries, including his own, and seek ways of transcending the limitations of ISI.[16] Regional integration and individual commodity agreements were only part of the answer. In addition Prebisch gave increasing emphasis to the need to reform the institutional framework of international trade and the notion of compensatory transfers to the South of the inequitable gains accuring to the North through changes in the terms of trade, and indeed these demands were to become central in the programme of the South.

Many vigorous attacks have been launched against the Prebisch thesis. The claim concerning secular deterioration of the terms of trade of third-world countries has been convincingly undermined by a generation of liberal economists.[17] Many of the analytical underpinnings supporting the empirical generalization have also been questioned. Yet even the most effective critic of the supposed long-term deterioration in terms of trade of primary commodities relative to manufactures finds that there was a very substantial deterioration from an admittedly advantageous position during the period 1950/5–1962/3, and is willing to concede that the first United Nations Conference on Trade and Development (UNCTAD), convened in the early 1960s, had every reason to be concerned about the problem. Between 1954 and 1962, the terms of trade between primary products and capital equipment in exchanges between developed and less developed states had deteriorated by 38 per cent, swallowing 'a very important fraction of the financial aid granted to the Third World'.[18] Furthermore, economists have been almost unanimous in observing, if only to deplore it, the way in which certain strands of the Prebisch doctrine have taken on a life of their own, unauthorized by their creator and impervious to reason.[19]

In short, whatever may be felt about the competence of Prebisch as an economist, the fact remains that his ideas were timely and remain immensely influential. Most of all, the notion of some automatic mechanism in world trade acting against the interests of the third world had immense intellectual appeal to minds trained within the liberal tradition but rebelling against it. It seemed to provide moral grounds for the long-independent Latin American states to demand compensation of the centre in the same tone and with the same confidence as new states, whose leaders could point to more specific and recent mercantilist distortions wrought in their economies by the imperial masters. Prebisch is evasive on this point, as it happens. At one point he argues that the tendency of countries at the centre to retain gains from their own technical progress 'does not mean that they are taking possession of something that does not belong to them'.[20] Later he comes to believe that 'countries experiencing a deterioration in the terms of trade have a prima-facie claim upon additional resources'.[21] But on this question, as on so many others, it is not what Prebisch wrote, but what politicians chose to believe him to have written that is important.[22] It is as orator even more than formal ideologue that Prebisch matters historically, then, and certainly not as economist, in which guise his main residual function seems to be as guy for the entertainment of pyrophiliac liberals. His most valuable single gift to the peoples of the Third World was an acceptable rationalization in the language of modern economics for their widespread feelings of resentment and powerlessness in the face of a rapidly changing external environment. With this psychological key in the lock, and the UN General Assembly under their control, the weak states of the world were poised for action.

Notes

1. PRO, FO 371/30503 A2021/181/51, Fraser to Gallop, 26 February 1942.
2. Asher Isaacs, *International Trade: Tariffs and Commercial Policies* (Chicago, Richard D. Irwin, 1948), pp. 269–73; Franklin R. Root, *International Trade and Investment* (4th edition, Cincinnati, Ohio, South-Western Publishing Co., 1978), pp. 165–71.
3. An interesting British Foreign Office minute of 19 March 1945 illustrates the continuing British fear of her overpowerful allies and provides a sidelight on the *political* as distinct from the more obvious commercial motives for British support for multilateralism. J. V. Perowne wrote, 'As I see it, the chief consequence of the war, from our point of view, will be that we shall have exchanged a more or less direct threat to our independence from Germany, Italy, and Japan for an even direr, if less immediate threat from Russia and the USA.' He advised that Britain should cultivate the satellites of the USA and encourage suitable European influences there. Multilateralism could serve as a check to the emergence of overwhelming United States hegemony in Latin America. (PRO FO 371/45012 AS 1599/176/51.)
4. Useful recent contributions to the literature on commercial policy in the 1930s include David E. Kaiser, *Economic Diplomacy and the Origins of the Second World War: Germany, Britain, France and Eastern Europe, 1930–1939* (Princeton, N.J., Princeton University Press, 1980); and Stanley E. Hilton, *Brazil and the Great Powers, 1930–1939: the Politics of Trade Rivalry* (Austin, Texas and London, University of Texas Press, 1975).
5. On differences in policy between Argentina, Australia, and Canada see Michael J. Twomey, 'Economic Fluctuations in Argentina, Australia, and Canada during the Depression of the 1930s' (unpublished paper presented to the International Congress of Americanists, Manchester, UK, September 1982). On military thinking in Argentina see Carl Solberg, 'Tariff and Politics in Argentina, 1916–1930', *Hispanic–American Historical Review*, 53, 2 (May, 1973), 260–84.
6. The transition from universalism to Atlanticism forms the principal theme of David P. Calleo and Benjamin M. Rowland, *America and the World Political Economy: Atlantic Dreams and National Realities* (Bloomington, Ind. and London, Indiana University Press, 1973); an interesting early account of the transition is to be found in the Woodrow Wilson Study Group (William Y. Elliott, chairman), *The Political Economy of American Foreign Policy: Its Concepts, Strategy, and Limits* (New York, Henry Holt and Co., 1955), pp. 201–34.

7. On the Nixon narcotics drive and its disastrous effects on Turkey see Nikolaos A. Stavrou, 'The Politics of Opium in Turkey' and Harvey R. Wellman, 'American Diplomacy and the International Narcotics Traffic', both in Luiz R. S. Simmons and Abdul A. Said, eds, *Drugs, Politics, and Diplomacy: the international connection* (Beverley Hills and London, Sage, 1974).

8. Brian Davey, *The Economic Development of India* (London, Spokesman Books, 1975), pp. 131, 145, 148; Vyuptakesh Sharan, 'Multinational Corporations and the Balance of Payments Problem in a Developing Host Country: an Indian Experience', *Indian Economic Journal*, 26 (1978), 199-215; M. C. Kapoor and Rajan Saxena, 'Taming the Multinationals in India', *Journal of World Trade Law*, 13 (1979), 170-8.

9. I. Little, Tibor Scitovsky and Maurice Scott, *Industry and Trade in Some Developing Countries: a Comparative Study* (Oxford, Oxford University Press, 1970); Bela Balassa, *et al.*, *The Structure of Protection in Developing Countries* (Baltimore, IBRD, Report No. EC-152, 1971); and, from Latin America, Celso Furtado, *Economic Development of Latin America: a Survey from Colonial Times to the Cuban Revolution* (Cambridge, Cambridge University Press, 1970) and, somewhat earlier, Raúl Prebisch, *Towards a New Trade Policy for Latin America* (New York, United Nations, 1964), see especially pp. 20-3.

10. This interpretation is persuasively presented in James F. Petras and Morris H. Morley, 'The Rise and Fall of Regionalism in the Andean Countries, 1969-1977', *Social and Economic Studies*, 27 (1978), 153-67. See especially p. 157.

11. Michael Leifer, 'The Paradox of ASEAN: a security organization without the structure of an alliance', *The Round Table*, 271 (1978), 261-8.

12. Pat Stortz, 'The Association of South-East Asian Nations: its development, achievements, and prospects' (unpublished MA dissertation, University of Warwick, 1979), Table 3.1, p. 63. Total intra-ASEAN trade as a percentage of total external trade of ASEAN states fell from 21.7 in 1967 to 17.9 in 1977.

13. Lars Anell and Birgitta Nygren, *The Developing Countries and the World Economic Order* (London, Frances Pinter, 1980).

14. Sydney D. Bailey, 'The UN Security Council: evolving practice', *The World Today*, 34 (1978), 100-6.

15. Economic Commission for Latin America, *The Economic Development of Latin America and its Principal Problems* (Lake Success, NY, United Nations Department of Economic Affairs, 1950); Raúl Prebisch, 'Commercial Policy in the Underdeveloped Countries', *American Economic Review*, 44 (1959), 251-73; *Towards a New Trade Policy for Development: report by the Secretary-General of the United Nations Conference on Trade and Development* (New York, United Nations, 1964). For summaries and evaluations see Luis Eugenio Di Marco, 'The Evolution of Prebisch's Economic Thought', in L. E. Di Marco, ed., *International Economics and Development: Essays in Honor of Raúl Prebisch* (New York and London, Academic Press Inc., 1972), pp. 3-13; M. June Flanders, 'Prebisch on Protectionism: an Evaluation', *Economic Journal*, 74 (1964), 305-26.

16. Prebisch spoke out strongly against the more extreme policies of ISI followed in the 1950s and stressed the complementary nature of agriculture and industry, as did other influential voices from the periphery at this time, including W. A. Lewis. See Raúl Prebisch, *Towards a New Policy*

for Development (New York, United Nations, 1964), pp. 20–2; W. A. Lewis, *Aspects of Industrialization* (Cairo, National Bank of Egypt, 1953), especially p. 19.

17. A number of critiques are reviewed in A. S. Friedeberg, *The United Nations Conference on Trade and Development of 1964* (Rotterdam, Rotterdam University Press, 1970), Chapter 3, 'The Theory of the Peripheral Economy'. See also John P. Powelson, 'The Strange Persistence of the "Terms of Trade" ', *Inter-American Economic Affairs*, 30 (1977), 17–28, and Paul Streeten, 'World Trade in Agricultural Commodities and the Terms of Trade with Industrial Goods' in Nurul Islam, ed., *Agricultural Policy in Developing Countries* (London, Macmillan, 1974).

18. Paul Bairoch, *The Economic Development of the Third World since 1900* (London, 1975), Chapter 6, 'The Terms of Trade', pp. 111–34.

19. Albert Fishlow, 'A New International Economic Order: What Kind?', in Fishlow, *et al.*, *Rich and Poor Nations in the World Economy* (New York, McGraw-Hill, 1978), p. 19; Powelson, 'The Strange Persistence of the "Terms of Trade" ', p. 17.

20. Raúl Prebisch, *Economic Survey of Latin America, 1949* (New York, United Nations, 1950), p. 55, quoted by Friedeberg, *The United Nations Conference on Trade and Development of 1964*, Chapter 3.

21. *Towards a New Trade Policy for Development* (New York, United Nations, 1964), p. 16.

22. Structuralist arguments after the manner of Prebisch are a far more common rationale for resource transfers than the colonial reparations claim which, as Craig MacPhee commented in a vigorous exchange with Martin Bronfenbrenner some years ago, 'has never been voiced in UNCTAD proceedings except by the Russians'. Typical is the crude allegation in a recent work sympathetic to UNCTAD doctrine, that 'the process of modernisation which began in Europe . . . and gave the countries which were industrialized at an early stage the political and economic dominion over the rest of the world is the principal cause of the injustices which lie behind the demands by the poor countries for a new international economic order' (M. Bronfenbrenner, 'Review Article: Predatory Poverty on the Offensive—the UNCTAD Record', *Economic Development and Cultural Change*, 24 (1976), 825–31; Craig R. MacPhee, 'Martin Bronfenbrenner on UNCTAD and the GSP; Comment' and M. Bronfenbrenner, 'Rejoinder to Professor MacPhee', *Economic Development and Cultural Change*, 27 (1979), 357–63, 365–6; Anell and Nygren, *The Developing Countries and the World Economic Order*, pp. 30–1).

2 THE INSTITUTIONS

The Bretton Woods System and its Shortcomings

Locating the source of their problems in the operation of the world economy as a whole might seem to have provided the LDCs with good reason to seek a collective solution in global forums. However the existing institutions with responsibility for the conduct of international economic affairs were firmly under the control of the industrialized West. Moreover, they had all too often been constituted and managed in ways which displeased third-world leaders.

The principal instruments of international economic management were three. The General Agreement on Tariffs and Trade, the International Monetary Fund, and the International Bank for Reconstruction and Development. None of these was addressed specifically to the problems of poor states. Instead the attention of their architects had been directed towards avoiding any repetition of the disasters of the inter-war period. Recovery and prosperity in Europe, full employment, exchange stability, and good trading relations between the major industrial economies seemed far more immediately important than the welfare of the LDCs.

The GATT had been founded upon principles of reciprocity and non-discrimination which many LDCs simply did not feel to be conducive to their economic development. Rightly or wrongly they agreed with Prebisch that 'however valid the most-favoured-nation principles may be in regulating trade relations among equals, it is not a suitable concept for trade involving countries of vastly unequal economic strength'.[1] Yet these principles were clearly expressed in entrenched clauses of the GATT, which could only be changed by a unanimous vote of the contracting parties.

But from a southern point of view the main practical problem about the GATT was that it operated in such a way that it was bound to be dominated by the preoccupations of the major trading nations. In tariff negotiations the range of goods subject to reduced duties was dictated by the main participants and reflected their trading schedules, not those of the LDCs; the problem was not dissimilar to that which had rendered the theoretically multilateral United States trade policy of the later 1930s rather less than multilateralist in practice. The concessions which resulted were indeed extended to all countries, even including non-signatories to the GATT, of which there were a great many in the Third World. Yet, because of the negotiating procedures, tariffs levied by the rich countries on manufactured goods imported from the South fell less rapidly than the generally lower tariffs which the rich imposed on manufactures exchanged between themselves.[2]

If GATT showed a bias towards matters of interest to major states, it also showed indifference to problems of the South. Nothing was done in the early years to correct the way in which the structure of DC tariffs effectively discouraged LDCs from processing primary products before exporting them. The raw material often entered free of duty; a tariff of 20 per cent on a derived article which had been doubled in value during processing was therefore, in effect, a tax of 40 per cent on the value added by the processing industry, and might often prove prohibitory. Nor was this all. When the GATT signatories broke their own rules by agreement it was admittedly sometimes in order to allow developing countries to increase import duties, but just as often it was to permit deviations of far greater quantitative import by the industrialized economies to the prejudice of southern interests. Thus waivers were granted to the USA in 1955 to allow continued agricultural protectionism, and, as noted earlier, the EEC countries were allowed to introduce a new system of preference in favour of their associated third-world states towards the end of the 1950s. In addition, the principal DCs had already, with the Long-Term Arrangement regarding Trade in Cotton Textiles (LTA) of 1962, set out along the path of negotiating voluntary quantitative restrictions on third-world exports that were alleged to be causing market disruption in the West. While this might just about be within the letter of the GATT and was duly legitimized, it clearly went against its spirit. And all this took place within an institution which many third-world countries felt to be a rich men's club, not even worth joining, and where, accordingly, amendments to the non-entrenched articles and waivers to permit special deviations from the rules could not be voted through by the same massive numbers which the South could summon up in the UN.

The IMF was no better. Hatched by the USA and Britain at Bretton Woods in 1944 and presented as a *fait accompli* to the rest of the world, the Fund was primarily intended to ensure the stability of the foreign exchanges and prevent damage to trade from competitive devaluations of the sort which had followed the devaluation of the US dollar in 1933. Each member state was assigned a quota which is paid into the Fund, partly in gold and partly in domestic currency. The quotas also dictated relative voting strength on the Executive Board which effectively managed the Fund as well as entitlement to borrow. Thus the United States, as the major participant, originally controlled almost 40 per cent of the votes, reduced by 1963 to just under 23 per cent, giving it in effect a built-in veto on many matters, including changes in quotas, which required a four-fifths majority.[3]

After the United States, the largest quotas in descending order of magnitude were originally allotted to Britain, China, France, and India. For various reasons the Fund was relatively inactive before 1956, but it began to assume a more important role thereafter. Yet by the mid-1960s Britain, the USA, India, France, and Brazil had together accounted for more than half the volume of drawings on the Fund even though, by this time, membership exceeded one hundred, many having joined as newly independent states since 1960. Moreover, four-fifths of the relatively small percentage of drawings made by the LDCs taken as a group had gone to just 10 per cent of their number, a good deal of it to India and Nationalist China. LDCs had little say in management and found that existing policy provided scant inducement to borrow even to assuage what were often very severe balance of payments difficulties.[4]

For one thing, these problems often stemmed in part from import-substituting industrialization strategies. Governments understood this very well and felt that the long-term benefits anticipated from such policies justified short-term inconvenience. Accordingly they resented being told to change to more open and deflationary policies by the US-dominated IMF. They resented it all the more since the IMF appeared to them to have taken insufficient account of structural differences between developed and underdeveloped countries.[5] On the one hand, third-world entitlements were understated in the quotas of the LDCs because these failed to give adequate weight to the greater variability of LDC as compared with DC export earnings. On the other hand, Fund officials at first appeared oblivious to the way in which demands for orthodox policies of deflation could affect economies with unsophisticated state apparatuses.[6] In the West, policy-makers had a wide range of fiscal and monetary tools to hand and could attack economic problems with a careful eye to political consequences. In most third-world countries, the tax system was primitive and inflexible so that attempts to comply with IMF conditions must all too often result in heavy-handed use of monetary policy. 'Monetary policy', one Brazilian economist complained, 'must create a permanent depression in order to keep the economy in equilibrium.'[7]

Finally there was the World Bank, or IBRD. Initially this had been directed rather more to post-war reconstruction in the belligerent states than to economic development, and when it did begin to look towards the Third World it proved inadequate in many ways. To begin with it loaned at market rates in hard currencies. Few projects in the least-developed countries could justify the burden this implied. Second, the Bank, like the IMF with which it often worked closely, imposed conditions on borrowers. It would not deal with states which were in default on past external loans, and it generally imposed policy conditions showing a bias towards private enterprise and openness of the economy, as, for example, in India in 1957.[8] Third, the funds at the disposal of the Bank were in no way sufficient to make a visible contribution to third-world development. Fourth, voting was in proportion to subscriptions, so that the USA, with 25.5 per cent of votes in 1966, could dominate the Bank in alliance with a handful of other DCs.

The creation of a soft-loan affiliate of the World Bank, the International Development Association (IDA), in 1960, went some way to meet these criticisms, and the World Bank group continued to be the predominant source of multilateral aid in spite of the emergence of new donor groups such as the EEC, the Organization of Arab Petroleum Exporting Countries (OAPEC), and regional development banks such as the Inter-American Development Bank founded in 1961 and the Asian Development Bank of 1968.[9] But multilaterally donated aid, though sometimes preferred by recipients because of its relative freedom from onerous restrictions and conditions and generally easier terms, has seldom exceeded a quarter of the total annual flow of aid to the Third World. The great bulk of financial assistance has been in the form of bilateral transfers of capital on more or less concessionary terms from countries such as the USA, Britain, and France. The flow of aid assumed large dimensions from the mid-1950s, but this proved to be a temporary and in many ways an unsatisfactory phenomenon, often having only the most remote connection with the process of economic development. Motivation is the key. Aid, in its myriad manifestations, acted as a conduit for great power strategic influence in the cold-war period, especially after 1956. Under Public Law 480 it provided an outlet for the costly surplus production of the protected US agricultural sector. Similarly, it was used to promote exports of only marginally viable industries such as armaments and shipbuilding by the governments of Britain, France, and the Soviet Union, to name but three.[10] Finally it was used to smooth over the wounds of decolonization. British bilateral aid, for example, more than doubled during the peak years between 1956 and 1963.[11]

Setting aside its accompanying rhetoric, aid may be seen all too often to have been primarily intended to assist the donor and to have done little for the recipient. Indeed opponents of aid, both Left and Right, have complained either of its irrelevance or, worse, of the harm it has done to the evolving structure of LDCs by substituting for and hence stunting local savings, or by skewing the development plans of recipients in the direction of the sorts of inappropriately capital-intensive or prestigious schemes preferred by donors.[12] Aid lingers on in spite of these criticisms and has in some degree responded to them, but the domestic economic problems of donor countries in the 1970s coupled with a gradual thaw in East–West relations and the end of the decolonization bulge of 1956–64 have brought the quantitative level down in relative terms. This has been most marked in the case of the USA where aid as a percentage of GNP fell from levels in excess of 0.5 in the early 1960s to 0.19 in 1979. The figures for France, another major donor, also show a marked drop, from 1.35 in 1960 to 0.59 in 1979.[13]

Southern Achievements in the UN to 1972: UNCTAD I–III

All in all the mood of the early 1960s may be summed up in this way. The world was experiencing unprecedentedly rapid and widespread economic growth, but states with low levels of per capita income were finding it relatively difficult to translate this into equitable improvements in living standards and the establishment of well-found and diversified productive structures. Growth did not automatically yield development, though US economists infuriatingly insisted on using the two terms as though synonymous.[14] Moreover the LDCs had come to believe that a principal source of their problems lay in the design and conduct of the western-dominated international economic institutions, a belief into which they had inadvertently been led by the leaders of the DCs themselves, who had come to believe unquestioningly in a strong causal connection between the GATT and the IMF on the one hand and the rise in international trade and living standards on the other. Since a number of other policy options were blocked, and since the great increase in their numbers favoured an initiative in international organizations where this might count for something, the attention of the LDCs turned to the UN as the obvious platform from which to launch a drive for reform.

This was not an entirely new tactic. During the early 1950s the LDCs had pressed unsuccessfully for an ambitious Special United Nations Fund for Economic Development (SUNFED), and though no body with so felicitous an acronym ever came into being, the campaign did yield in 1959 a United Nations Special Fund of modest dimensions to finance feasibility studies and other preparatory work and so improve the access of poorer countries to the major sources of aid.[15] But no real breakthrough came until the early 1960s, when calls for a major trade conference in the UN General Assembly and at the July 1962 Conference on Problems of Developing Countries in Cairo led the Economic and Social Committee of the UN (ECOSOC) to establish a preliminary committee to prepare for and convene the first United Nations Conference on Trade and Development (UNCTAD), which met in Geneva in 1964.[16]

It has long been conventional in the United States and Western Europe to deplore UNCTAD as unwieldy, unnecessary, and ineffective, yet it has undoubtedly been the central institution of the North–South dialogue over the past twenty years and has assumed great symbolic importance. Its evaluation is no simple matter.

How is one to rate the achievement of UNCTAD during its first decade, from the appointment of Prebisch as Secretary-General early in 1963 to the third full meeting of the Conference in Santiago de Chile in 1972? To begin with there is the fact that UNCTAD survived by securing its institutionalization as a permanent organ of the UN General Assembly. As such it has a standing committee of fifty-five members, the Trade and Development Board, meeting twice a year and reporting to the Assembly through ECOSOC between plenary sessions, and an apparatus of committees on commodities, trade in manufactured goods, invisibles and the financing of trade, institutional arrangements, the implications of regional integration, and shipping, all serviced by a permanent secretariat in Geneva. This was done in the face of opposition from the USA and other DCs, which felt that the matters proposed for discussion by Prebisch and the South could more easily be dealt with in existing forums, such as the GATT, with clear and established decision-making procedures, than in a massive UN conference with thousands of participants working on the principle of one-state-one-vote.

Second, UNCTAD managed against all the odds to evolve ways of transacting business in spite of its universal membership. From the start it succeeded in aggregating the interests of its large membership into a manageable number of conflicting views, so that agreements of a sort—loosely drafted and hedged about with demurrers—could be reached. This was done by concerting positions on agenda items within groups prior to negotiation. The formal purpose of the four groups was the election of representatives to the Trade and Development Board. Group A included all African and Asian states together with Yugoslavia. At the time of UNCTAD I these numbered sixty-one, and were allotted twenty-two seats on the Board. Group B, with eighteen seats, consisted of the twenty-nine DCs. Group C, the Latin American republics, elected nine representatives, while the centrally-planned economies of COMECON were given six Board members. In effect, however, groups A and C very soon united in the Group of 77, so called because it originally had that many members. A handful of states, including some significant participants in the wider process of North–South relations such as South Africa and Cuba, belonged to no group and were therefore effectively excluded from playing their part in proceedings.[17] So, in sharp contrast to the Bretton Woods institutions, UNCTAD was dominated from the start by a coalition of LDCs with a permanent voting majority in spite of the fact that well over half its budget was subscribed by the Group B states.

The group system simplified negotiations within UNCTAD by ensuring that the largest and most influential states were always represented on the Board and in important committees. As might be expected, quantitative work by Joseph Nye confirms that 'the countries that ranked higher in influence in UNCTAD than would have been expected from their power in the general environment were less-developed countries such as Brazil, India, Chile, the UAR, Yugoslavia, and Nigeria', all with relatively extensive and mature administrative systems, while the states with the greatest influence in absolute terms were considered to be France, the USA, and the UK. On the whole, the influence of the third-world countries was directed towards sponsorship of new proposals, sometimes at the behest of the secretariat, while the power of the DCs was used to block and veto. But this was not the whole of the story, for France ranked fifth among the mainly LDC initiators, while Brazil ranked tenth among the blockers.

If the group system helped to aggregate interests and clarify positions this might of course lead just as easily to arid confrontation as to fruitful negotiation, and indeed firm treaty-like agreements have been slow to emerge within UNCTAD. To this end, potentially counter-productive rigidity of the group system has been mollified by the emergence of broker states, including some of the third-world leaders listed above, and sympathetic smaller North European countries such as Sweden. Small contact groups of delegates from these states meeting hard against deadlines have sometimes been able to resolve disagreements.[18]

Self-perpetuation and institution-building may be worthy goals for the bureaucrat, but they cut little ice in the world at large. Yet if one searches for more concrete results of the early years of UNCTAD they are few, because the Group B countries were extremely reluctant to commit themselves. The first substantive achievement of the new forum was an agreement at UNCTAD II, which met in New Delhi in 1968, to move toward the establishment of generalized systems of preference (GSPs) in favour of the LDCs, and many rich states including the USA and the EEC did introduce schemes of this kind over the next eight years. But all the GSPs introduced by the DCs were so hedged about with exclusions, qualifications, and non-tariff barriers of one sort and another that they were only pale shadows of the original concept advanced by Prebisch in the previous decade. Delhi also saw the beginnings of the integrated programme for commodities (IPC), which was to become the centrepiece of UNCTAD negotiations in the mid-1970s. Finally, the DCs were persuaded reluctantly to agree to aid targets without clearly defined timetables, which they subsequently fell well short of in response to domestic pressures.

UNCTAD III, which took place at Santiago in 1972, was described by one delegate as 'a gigantic farce'.[19] Minor achievements included the creation of a third-world Group of 20 to represent the views of the LDCs in the counsels of the IMF, and agreement on a number of principles favourable to the interests of the Third World which were to govern the forthcoming round of multilateral trade negotiations (MTN) under the GATT.[20] However the general mood was one of disillusion at the lack of tangible achievements. 'UNCTAD III produced no decisions to make immediate and substantial changes in trade, aid, or monetary matters which would benefit the developing countries'.[21]

The General Agreement on Tariffs and Trade

There were also those who took the more subtle but ultimately no less pessimistic view that UNCTAD ought not to be judged as a quasi-legislature and consigned to oblivion because it had not come up with fresh rules. R. S. Walters argued that the political party, as 'articulator, aggregator and communicator of interests is a more appropriate analogue to the role UNCTAD is performing in international politics than is Congress with its coercive, rule-making powers'.[22] He went on to maintain that UNCTAD had in fact succeeded in its chief task, which had been to capture the attention of key northern bureaucrats and policy-makers.[23] Joseph Nye echoed this view, recalling almost with approval how the acronym had been adapted to stand for 'Under No Circumstances Take Any Decision'.[24] Its object had been to establish 'a new set of economic norms' by constant reiteration, and to prophesy, less in the sense of foretelling the future than of explaining and bearing witness to the truth.[25]

On this view, UNCTAD would have to be judged not simply by its own short-run substantive achievements but rather by the extent to which it succeeded in changing the tone of relations between North and South across the board. In making any such assessment there are naturally very substantial obstacles. It is not easy to determine how far a softening of attitudes towards third-world problems in the IMF, for example, may have stemmed from changes peculiar to that institution, from the publicity effect of UNCTAD, or from a much more general drift of attention towards third-world problems of which UNCTAD itself was but one facet. This said, a prima facie case may be made. There were indications of change in the quality of North–South relations during the 1960s in the GATT, in the IMF, in the management of international trade in some primary commodities, and in the relations of the EEC with its Associated States. These will be examined in turn.

The GATT may not have been designed with third-world development in mind, but as early as the end of the 1950s, before UNCTAD was summoned, the contracting parties had begun to show concern for the problems of the LDCs. The Haberler Report of 1958 called for expansion of exports from poorer countries, and a ministerial meeting of the GATT in October of that year responded by setting up a working party to identify impediments to trade in commodities of special interest to the LDCs and to consider how these might be removed. Further action was taken at the 1963 ministerial meeting which inaugurated the Kennedy Round of multilateral trade negotiations (MTNs). The Kennedy Round was to have as one of its objectives the unreciprocated reduction of DC barriers to LDC exports. Besides this the ministers of the member states agreed on further moves in favour of the LDCs which were finally drafted in the form of an addition to the Agreement itself, known as Part IV. By adopting Part IV of the GATT, which came into effect formally in June 1966, the DCs engaged themselves to try to avoid increasing barriers against the exports of LDCs any further and, where possible, to reduce them. They also established an International Trade Centre at Geneva to provide information and training facilities for officials. The progress of initiatives stemming from these provisions was to be watched over by a new GATT committee on Trade and Development.[26] Finally, towards the end of the 1960s, the GATT sanctioned the GSPs demanded by the Third World through UNCTAD.

All these developments took place during the very years that UNCTAD was coming into being. To some extent they met the criticisms which had fuelled UNCTAD. Yet they left intact the labyrinthine apparatus of high-cost protected temperate-zone agriculture, the levying of revenue taxes by DC governments on mildly addictive goods such as tea, coffee, and tobacco, and the growing network of subsidies and other non-tariff barriers that was springing up in the older industrial economies as governments strove to shore up ageing textile, steel, and allied industries under the rather thin pretence of restructuring to meet changed patterns of international comparative advantage. The objectionable textiles LTA of 1962, for example, originally rationalized as a transitional measure, was twice extended in 1967 and 1970, so institutionalizing a system of quite explicit quantitative controls of the sort the GATT had been pledged to outlaw.

The International Monetary Fund

In the IMF, too, moves to meet the demands of the LDCs antedated UNCTAD I. As early as 1952 the incoming Managing Director of the Fund, Ivar Routh, had made possible some liberalization of the lending policy of the IMF by introducing short-term standby credits, which would not only be made available more quickly than past drawings but could also be negotiated individually on each occasion and might therefore, in principle, be adapted to the necessities of weaker economies. In 1956 the second quinquennial review of quotas had found those of a number of small states to be inadequate, and a small quota policy had been introduced whereby these could be increased by anything up to 100 per cent in accord with a prescribed formula.[27] Taken together with general quota increases and specific increases unconnected with it, such as those of Egypt and Iran in 1948, the effect of the small quota policy by 1970 had been to increase the quotas of the twenty-five LDC founders by an average of 183 per cent, as compared with an increase of 109 per cent in DC quotas.[28]

More obviously useful to LDCs than either of these permissive reforms were the introduction of Special Drawing Rights (SDRs) in 1969 and of the IMF Compensatory Finance Facility (CFF) in 1963.

In 1969 the IMF created a new unit, the SDR. Over the next three years 9.5 billion SDRs were allocated to members in proportion to their IMF quotas. The value of the SDR was originally fixed in terms of gold, and later with reference to a basket first of sixteen and subsequently of five major trading currencies. As one chronicler of international finance has observed,

The SDR is neither credit nor money. Rather, and more confusingly, it is credit money. It is money because it is a fiduciary instrument governed in its use by intricate and precise legal instruments which have force in international law. It is credit because it represents a claim on the liquid assets of others. It is not exactly money because it cannot be used entirely freely; it is not exactly credit because it is virtually automatically convertible into money.[29]

The political significance of SDRs was quite simple. They represented an attempt to introduce a degree of rationality and equity into the determination and allocation of international liquidity, a revival, though on a rather modest scale, of Keynes's visionary proposal of the 1940s for a world currency. Over the past two decades the only sources of increased liquidity had been newly mined gold and US deficits, neither of which could be subjected either to effective international political control or to satisfactorily reliable market determination. Now this position was changed in principle by a new interest-bearing reserve asset, which could be used for payments between central banks and in transactions with the IMF, and which each member of the IMF agreed to accept up to a level three times its own national allocation. LDCs were quick to point out that a concessional element could be introduced into the world monetary system by fiddling with the allocation rules governing SDRs, for example, by channelling rich countries' allocations to the LDCs via the World Bank and the regional development banks.[30] The function of SDRs consequently became an item on the North–South agenda during the 1970s.

The CFF lacked the broad macroeconomic intellectual appeal of the SDR. It was designed to make additional funds available to countries which could demonstrate that their balance of payments problems arose from abnormally variable export earnings. The scheme worked like this. Countries whose current export earnings fell more than an agreed percentage below a specified level were able to draw up to 25 per cent, later increased by stages to 100 per cent, of the value of their IMF quota to compensate for the decline. The IMF had, of course, to be satisfied that there was no question of a decline having been engineered deliberately, as part of an industrialization programme, say, and this meant that as with other IMF drawings there was a strong element of scrutiny and conditionality. Moreover, in the event CFF drawings tended often to be made in place of ordinary IMF drawings, though they had been intended to supplement these.

But this was not the worst of it. The level against which short-falls were measured was the average for a five-year period of which the shortfall year was the centre. This figure was clearly dependent for its accuracy on techniques of estimation and forecasting, since definitive figures could not possibly be available for more than two of the five years in question; and here lay a major weakness of the scheme. Finger and Derosa have established that in less than 50 per cent of cases where CFF drawings were authorized did it finally turn out that export earnings for the year in question *had* in fact been below the long-term trend. In their view this understandable in-accuracy was the most powerful reason why the CFF, in spite of outstanding drawings in the region of $4 billion, had had no discern-ible effect on the stability of export earnings in the seventy-one countries that had resorted to it up to the late 1970s. In defence of the Facility it could be argued that, while it did not solve the prob-lem of export earnings instability, it did the next best thing by effectively—though by the most roundabout route imaginable—enlarging the IMF quotas of LDCs (but not their voting power). It had given assistance where vagaries of the commodity trades posed a recurrent threat to development in a way that avoided the poten-tially damaging rows over issues of principle which would surely have attended any attempt to redraft the criteria governing deter-mination of IMF quotas.[31]

Yet even this laudably realistic rationalization of the CFF fails if the premise concerning the alleged link between instability of export earnings and rate of economic growth can be broken. And a number of economists have argued that, contrary to expectation, there is a *positive* correlation between export earnings instability and growth in the percentage of GNP invested.[32] This leaves only the Jesuitically casuistic defence that, precisely because it fails in its alleged inten-tion, the CFF at least does no *harm* to the investment ratio of recipients.

Individual Commodity Agreements: Coffee, Sugar, Tin

It might appear that a more direct way to attack the problems of primary producers would have been to stabilize trade through individual commodity agreements. The Brazilians, overwhelmingly the largest producers of coffee, had borrowed huge sums in the early decades of the twentieth century in an attempt to keep coffee prices off the floor in periods of glut. In the 1930s they had tried without success to persuade other Latin American producers to co-operate with them. The main result of their policy by mid-century had been a very substantial decline in the Brazilian share of the world market as competitors in Latin America and Africa hitched a free ride on their more disciplined contemporaries. Tighter demand in the late forties and early fifties brought higher prices but in the absence of any form of regulation it led also to extensive planting of new bushes, threatening oversupply towards the end of the decade. This stimulus at last brought international co-operation as the Latin American Coffee Agreement of 1958 was extended to embrace producers in the British and Portuguese empires before being re-negotiated in 1961 as a near-universal five-year agreement under UN auspices.[33]

Sugar was another product of interest to a number of the poorest states. Here international agreement had been reached by the major exporters in reaction to depressed market conditions after the Crash of 1929. Like the Brazilians, the major producer signatories to the 1931 Chadbourne Agreement soon found themselves outflanked by new producers. Further agreements to regulate the free-market price were concluded in 1954 and 1958. Each failed to defend the price range it had sought to establish as sugar first soared at the time of Suez and later collapsed in 1959. The bulk of international trade in sugar was regulated by long-term fixed-price agreements between exporting and importing states, so that the extreme volatility of the free market is easily explained by its highly residual character. If one year's crop were sufficient to meet long-term contracts for 6 million tonnes and still leave as much again for the free market, an increase of eight per cent in exports from 12 to 13 million tonnes the next year would represent (disregarding stocks) a growth of almost 17 per cent in the amount coming on to the free market, with a proportionate effect on prices. This helps to account for the pattern of the early 1960s, when sugar more than doubled in price from a very low level of 2 US cents per lb. during 1962 and shot up to almost 12 cents per lb. in 1963 before falling back to below 4 cents per lb. the following year. In these circumstances the selection of sugar for the first major commodity negotiations under UNCTAD auspices in 1965 was a very stiff challenge.

The 1965 sugar conference was not a success. LDCs with good long-term arrangements with the USA or under the Commonwealth Sugar Agreement were not able to agree with less privileged and poorer producers. But a second UNCTAD sugar conference held shortly after UNCTAD II in 1968 did establish an agreement to run until 1973. Importing states undertook not to buy from countries outside the agreement when the market was weak and only to go beyond their traditional levels of purchase from these countries when prices rose above 5.25 US cents per lb. In exchange, exporters agreed to assure regular supplies by holding substantial stocks at their own expense. LDCs were given three special concessions. As prices rose from the floor of 3.25 cents per lb. and the quotas of exporters were raised, the shortfall arising through any exporter being unable to take full advantage of the enlarged quotas was to be distributed among the other exporters in a way that gave preference to LDCs. Secondly, LDCs were allowed to keep smaller stocks than DC exporters. Thirdly, some element of preference to LDCs was present in the criteria for fixing basic export quotas.[34]

A third primary commodity brought within an ICA by the late 1960s was tin. Like sugar, tin had been regulated in the 1930s by international agreement between major exporters. The output controls and buffer stock of the 1930s were not revived in the immediate post-war period, but in 1956 a five-year International Tin Agreement was reached between most non-Communist producers and all major importers bar the USA. Regular renewal made this the most venerable and apparently successful of the ICAs by the end of the sixties, and although the USA stayed out, the USSR finally joined the fourth ITA in 1971. By this time, tin, sugar, and coffee were beginning to seem like the harbingers of a general move toward international regulations of commodity markets as further agreements were reached for tea (1969), cocoa (1970), and sisal and henequen (1970).

Optimists about international organization might well conclude from this that commodity agreements were progressively taming the notoriously volatile markets on which some of the world's poorest countries depended for the bulk of their foreign exchange earnings. They would be wrong. In no case can it be shown that a commodity agreement succeeded in stabilizing prices. The coffee agreement succeeded in keeping prices substantially above costs of production for a short period, acting as an indirect and imprecise form of aid from the USA to Latin America. Yet this quite deliberate US subsidy, designed to secure political support and isolate the fledgling socialist regime in Cuba, had unintended effects which were bound, in the long run, to destabilize the market. The 1968 sugar agreement fell well short of the demands of the LDCs. They had tried without success to secure reductions in high-cost beet production in temperate-zone countries, and the dumping of surplus, subsidized beet-derived sugar on the world market. But in the end the principal culprit, the EEC, failed even to join the agreement and offered no guarantee whatsoever that it would abide by the 300,000 ton export quota alloted to it. Nor did the agreement touch on another major determinant of the market, the Cuban question. At the end of 1960, following the rupture in US–Cuban relations, United States imports of Cuban sugar ceased. Since Cuba was the largest single exporter, and since the USA had formerly been the biggest buyer of Cuban sugar, this strategically-motivated action had considerable impact on the market. The USA increased imports from other Latin American suppliers but also raised domestic production of protected beet sugar, threatening to reduce still further the percentage of world production traded internationally on the free market and so driving the price down to less than two cents per lb., well below the production cost of the most efficient suppliers. Cuba withdrew its co-operation from the international agreement because other signatories would not increase its free market quota to compensate for the loss of its bilateral arrangement with the USA and started to sell to the planned economies instead, whence some of the large Cuban output leaked out intermittently on to the free market in search of hard currencies.[35] Finally it is apparent from recent work that the apparently causal relation between regularly renewed tin agreements and the relatively stable behaviour of the market for tin was largely coincidental. It was the US government which stabilized tin prices by net sales of 120,000 tons from its immense strategic stockpile over the period 1956–74, knocking the top off potential price booms between 1963 and 1966 and from 1973 to 1974. On both occasions the International Tin Council used up its entire stocks and was powerless to prevent further price rises.[36]

The three pre-1968 ICAs covering products of special interest to third-world exporters turn out on examination to have been little more than froth on the surface of markets in which real strength lay with the major consumer countries, most of all with the USA, and where strategic motives were constantly at work. Nor were there any clear signs that market forces might upset the prevailing pessimism about the secular tendency of primary commodity prices. Taking 1960—itself not an especially buoyant year—as base, the price indexes for tropical foods and beverages and vegetable oils and seeds stood at 99 in 1968 after eight relatively uneventful years. The index for agricultural raw materials had declined steadily to 68, and only ores and minerals had exhibited any real buoyancy, rising to 153 in 1966 only to fall back again to 130 by 1968, a phenomenon which could be partly explained away by the effects of political conflicts in Southern Africa and labour disputes in Chile on the supply and price of copper.[37]

The EEC and its Associates in the Third World: Yaoundé I and II

Relations between the EEC states and their former dependencies in the Third World provide a last area in which considerable institutional innovation was taking place in the 1960s. Article 131 of the Treaty of Rome, by which the Community was formed on the eve of African decolonization in 1957, provided for a special status of association with eighteen territories outside Europe. Following independence the terms of this relationship were renegotiated in the form of a convention signed in July 1963 at Yaoundé, in the Cameroon. The associated territories were the Malagassy Republic, Somalia, Zaïre, the tiny states of Rwanda and Burundi, and twelve former French dependencies in Africa south of the Maghreb.

The Yaoundé Convention included an agreement in principle to remove trade barriers between each associate and the six EEC countries and provide access to two new multilateral aid sources, the European Development Fund and the European Investment Bank. In addition a system of governmental and democratic institutions was set up to watch over the working of the Convention, including an Association Committee of civil servants, an annual Parliamentary Conference bringing together members of the European Assembly and of equivalent bodies in the Associated states, a Court of Arbitration, and an annual ministerial Council of Association. Last, as a concession to other LDCs, including populous former dependencies in South-East Asia and elsewhere which had been declared non-associable, the EEC introduced reductions in its common external tariff for tropical goods including coffee, tea, and cocoa.

A further reduction of the common external tariff took place in response to lobbying by the Non-Associables at UNCTAD II when the Yaoundé Convention was renegotiated for a further five years in 1969. At the same time the amount of aid available was increased, and there was a little easing of access for tropical products such as oilseeds and sugar which competed with European domestic production covered by the protectionist Common Agricultural Policy (CAP).

From the point of view of the Associated States Yaoundé II no less than Yaoundé I exhibited serious deficiencies in practice. The agreement to remove trade barriers was so hedged about with caveats as to be meaningless. The EEC gave privileged access only to products which it needed and could not produce itself. To add to the list of products entering the EEC free required a unanimous vote of the Council of Association, as did the *deletion* of any item from the list of EEC products allowed free into the Associates. The EEC tariff structure effectively penalized LDC industries engaged in processing or packing goods on the free list such as tea or coffee. Furthermore, while the Conventions multilateralized many favourable regulations governing capital flows as well as trade which had formerly been extended only to the colonial power, they did nothing to open up new economic relations between the eighteen Associates, in spite of their contiguity. Finally, aid provided under the Conventions was sluggishly disbursed at the arbitrary discretion of the European Commission and often served to help producers adapt production to the loss of privileged colonial arrangements above world prices, an adjustment effectively forced on the Associated by their former masters in the first place.

To many critics, then, the Yaoundé Conventions were simply a neo-colonialist device which showed that imperialism had remained true to itself. 'Its real face is unchanged under the mask', alleged one. 'The system which has been set up is only the old colonial pact, softened just sufficiently to mislead people.'[38]

The drift of events during the 1960s can therefore hardly be said to support the attractive and ingenious view that UNCTAD operated indirectly upon North–South relations, preaching a message and stimulating action which was ultimately taken in other forums. Many of the relevant developments elsewhere preceded UNCTAD I, and it would be straining credibility too much to suggest that they were primarily anticipatory concessions aimed at disarming UNCTAD. With the exception of the creation of the SDR, such reforms as took place in the GATT, at the IMF, and at the time of decolonization in French and Belgian Africa were well under way if not completed by 1964.

Changes in World Bank policy and in the commodity markets are another matter. The shift away from project aid toward programme aid owed a good deal to the adoption of proposals originally voiced in UNCTAD I for a Supplementary Finance Facility (SFF) to project agreed LDC economic plans against shortfalls in export earnings, but for a number of reasons this found little favour with prospective clients.[39] Prebisch had suggested an instrument along the lines of the SDR in his 1964 report, and the question had subsequently been discussed within UNCTAD.[40] It is less easy to tell how much, if anything, the easing of IBRD terms after 1963 owed to pressure emanating from UNCTAD. As for the early ICAs, only that governing sugar had originated in UNCTAD-sponsored negotiations, but this was clearly a direction in which the new organization felt it could achieve positive results in the short to medium term.

This said, it was doubtful how easily UNCTAD would be able to shift from its initial prophetic posture to a negotiating role. Some felt that the very qualities which made UNCTAD an effective voice made it an ineffective forum for detailed negotiation.[41] The group system seemed to favour confrontation and declamation rather than co-operation and diplomacy. Besides, if UNCTAD were to become an effective decision-maker, the smaller LDCs would suffer by their inability to provide enough trained officials to cover all the parallel sessions of regional groups and sub-groups, committees, and working groups which continued day and night through full sessions of the Conference.[42] Furthermore it seemed all too likely that the mood of confidence needed for productive talks in committee could be broken by the hail of missiles from the plenary sessions, where the flow of rhetoric continued unabated. Would the UNCTAD secretariat or the leaders of the Group of 77 be able to lift their artillery barrage before their troops stormed up the beaches?

UNCTAD, like many other initiatives of the early years of the first UN development decade, seemed to have lost a great deal of its initial momentum by the end of the decade. After UNCTAD III in 1972 it was easy to take the view that 'international bargaining of the UNCTAD kind is not likely to retain its present importance', and to accept that

> political differences among the developing countries are likely to increase, and their views concerning their relationship with the rich industrialized world will so divide them that it will be impossible to formulate unified demands. An increasing number of radical developing countries will move towards a more restricted relationship with the developed world, while the larger, more powerful and less radical developing countries and regional groupings will find it easier to strike their own bilateral bargains.[43]

This forecast, so reasonable at the time, could hardly have been more wrong. The next few years were to be the heyday of North–South negotiations, characterized by solidarity of the Group of 77 in spite of differences of interest between its members. Such radical governments as survived showed a disconcerting tendency to forge strong trade and debt relations with the West in spite of any ideological differences. It is time to explain how this extraordinary revolution came about.

Notes

1. *Towards a New Trade Policy for Development: Report by the Secretary-General of the United Nations Conference on Trade and Development* (New York, United Nations, 1964), p. 66.
2. B. Balassa, *The Structure of Protection in Industrial Countries* (IBRD Report No. EC-152), cited in Hans Singer and Javed Ansari, *Rich and Poor Countries* (London, George Allen & Unwin, 1977), p. 80, Table 5.1.
3. Hans Aufricht, *The International Monetary Fund: Legal Bases, Structure, Functions* (London, Stevens & Sons, 1964), p. 42.
4. Susan Strange, 'IMF: Monetary Managers', in Robert W. Cox and Harold K. Jacobson, *et al.*, *The Anatomy of Influence: Decision Making in International Organization* (New Haven and London, Yale University Press, 1973), p. 267.
5. Graham Bird, 'Financial Flows to Developing Countries: the Role of the International Monetary Fund', *Review of International Studies*, 7 (1981), p. 93; Aufricht, *The International Monetary Fund*, pp. 35-6.
6. Two spirited attacks on the record of the Bretton Woods institutions were published in the early 1970s. Cheryl Payer, *The Debt Trap: the IMF and the Third World* (Harmondsworth, Penguin, 1974), as the title suggests, deals solely with the IMF, while the pungent critique of Teresa Hayter, *Aid as Imperialism* (Harmondsworth, Penguin, 1971), extends to the World Bank as well. Susan Strange, less histrionic in tone, notes that gradually 'the original simplistic Fund orthodoxy, which held that all a primary-producing country had to do was fight against inflation, became eroded through contact with the political problems of policy making for economic development', though she does not date this transformation. There is no sign in more recent work of Teresa Hayter that she accepts any such change for the better (Strange: 'IMF: Monetary Managers' in Cox and Jacobson, *et al.*, *The Anatomy of Influence*, p. 275; Teresa Hayter, *The Creation of World Poverty: an Alternative View to the Brandt Report* (London, Pluto, 1981), pp. 82-96).
7. Celso Furtado, *Economic Development of Latin America: a survey from colonial times to the Cuban revolution* (Cambridge, Cambridge University Press, 1970), p. 74.
8. See Chapter 1, above at note 8. More generally, see Hayter, *Aid as Imperialism*. For a more sympathetic account of the World Bank, see Roy Blough, 'The World Bank Group', *International Organization*, 22 (1968), 152-81, also reprinted in Richard N. Gardner and Max F. Millikan, eds, *The Global Partnership: international agencies and economic development* (New York, Praeger, 1968). Blough also notes disagreements on policy with Turkey and Brazil, but is inclined to be more cynical than Hayter about the underlying motives of third-world governments.
9. On the origins of the development banks see Henry Simon Bloch, 'Regional Development Financing', *International Organization*, 22 (1968), 182-203, reprinted in Gardner and Millikan, eds, *The Global Partnership*.
10. On arms exports from the Soviet Union see Raymond Hutchings, 'Soviet Arms Exports to the Third World: a Pattern and its Implications', *The World Today* (October 1978), 378-89. For Britain and France see Stockholm International Peace Research Institute, *The Arms Trade with the Third World* (Harmondsworth, Penguin, 1975), pp. 100-39. General treatments of aid which deal with the political motivations include Charles R.

Frank, Jr, and Mary Baird, 'Foreign Aid: Its Speckled Past and Future Prospects', *International Organization*, 29 (1975), 133–67.

11. Edward S. Mason and Robert S. Asher, *The World Bank since Bretton Woods* (Washington D.C., Brookings Institute, 1973), cited in Joan E. Spero, *The Politics of International Economic Relations* (London, Allen & Unwin, 1978), p. 140.

12. For a stimulating view from the liberal right see P. T. Bauer, *Dissent on Development* (student edition, London, Weidenfeld & Nicolson Ltd., 1976), pp. 95–135.

13. *World Development Report*, 1981 (New York, IBRD, 1981), p. 164, Table 16.

14. H. W. Arndt, 'Economic Development: a Semantic History', *Economic Development and Cultural Change*, 29 (1981), p. 465.

15. Spero, *The Politics of International Economic Relations*, p. 136; and see Robert E. Asher, Walter M. Kotschnig, William Adams Brown, Jr, *et al.*, *The United Nations and Economic and Social Cooperation* (Washington D.C., The Brookings Institution, 1957).

16. UNCTAD, itself wordy to a fault, has generated a considerable secondary literature as well. A short and businesslike early account of its founding and first meeting is to be found in Michael Zammit Cutajar and Alison Franks, *The Less Developed Countries in World Trade* (London, ODI Ltd, 1967), Chapters 9 and 10. A. S. Friedeberg, *The United Nations Conference on Trade and Development* (Rotterdam, Rotterdam University Press, 1969) is useful, as are Richard N. Gardner, 'The United Nations Conference on Trade and Development', *International Organization*, 22 (1968), 99–130, reprinted in Gardner and Millikan, eds, *The Global Partnership*; Joseph S. Nye, 'UNCTAD: poor nations' pressure group', in Cox and Jacobson, *et al.*, *The Anatomy of Influence*, pp. 334–70; and, for chronology, R. Krishnamurti, 'UNCTAD as a Negotiating Institution', *Journal of World Trade Law*, 15 (1981), 3–40.

17. Nye, 'UNCTAD: poor nations' pressure group', in Cox and Jacobson *et al.*, *The Anatomy of Influence*, p. 356.

18. Ibid.

19. Ann Zammit, 'UNCTAD III: End of an Illusion', *IDS Bulletin* (Sussex), 5 (1973), p. 3.

20. Ibid., pp. 11–12.

21. Ibid., p. 6.

22. R. S. Walters, 'International Organization and Political Communication: the use of UNCTAD by less developed countries', *International Organization*, 25 (1971), p. 821.

23. Ibid., p. 826.

24. Nye, 'UNCTAD', in Cox and Jacobson *et al.*, *The Anatomy of Influence*, p. 334.

25. Ibid., p. 345. This view of UNCTAD in the 1960s as pressure group, publicist, and prophet seems to have become an orthodoxy. It is repeated for example in Javed Ansari, 'Environmental Characteristics and Organizational Ideology: UNCTAD and the lessons of 1964', *British Journal of International Studies*, 4 (1978), 135–60.

26. Cutajar and Franks, *The Less Developed Countries in World Trade*, Chapter 8.

27. Aufricht, *The International Monetary Fund*, p. 37.

28. Strange, 'IMF: Monetary Managers', in Cox and Jacobson *et al.*, *The Anatomy of Influence*, p. 278.
29. Duncan Cameron, 'Special Drawing Rights', *International Journal*, 36 (1981), p. 724.
30. Singer and Ansari, *Rich and Poor Countries*, p. 186.
31. J. M. Finger and Dean A. Derosa, 'The Compensatory Finance Facility and Export Instability', *Journal of World Trade Law*, 14 (1980), 14–22.
32. Alasdair I. MacBean, *Export Instability and Economic Development* (Glasgow, Allen & Unwin, 1966), cited in L. Anell and B. Nygren, op. cit., pp. 141–2.
33. J. W. F. Rowe, *Primary Commodities in International Trade* (Cambridge, Cambridge University Press, 1965), pp. 177–83.
34. Ibid., pp. 174–7; F. O. Grogan, *International Trade in Temperate Zone Products* (Edinburgh, Oliver & Boyd, 1972), Chapter 6; Ian Smith, 'Sugar Markets in Disarray', *Journal of World Trade Law*, 9 (1975), 41–62.
35. Grogan, *International Trade in Temperate Zone Products*, p. 121.
36. G. W. Smith and G. R. Schink, 'The International Tin Agreement: a Reassessment', *Economic Journal*, 86 (1976), 715–28.
37. Carmine Nappi, *Commodity Market Controls: a Historical Review* (Lexington, Mass., Lexington Books, 1979), p. 19, Table 2.10. The table is based on UNCTAD data; the indexes are based on current US $ prices and exclude sales under long-term contracts or at preferential prices.
38. Pierre Jalée, *The Pillage of the Third World* (Paris, 1965; English translation by Mary Kopper, New York and London, Monthly Review Press, 1968), p. 96.
39. Roy Blough, 'The World Bank Group', *International Organization*, 22 (1968), 158–9; Singer and Ansari, *Rich and Poor Countries*, pp. 127–8.
40. *Towards a New Trade Policy for Development: report by the General-Secretary of the United Nations Conference.*
41. Walters, 'International Organization and Political Communication', pp. 832–3.
42. Zammit, 'UNCTAD III: End of an Illusion', pp. 7–8.
43. Ibid., p. 13.

3 THE DIALOGUE TRANSFORMED?

The Dual Crisis: Dollars and Oil

The dramatic suddenness of the rise in oil prices which galvanized the creaking dialogue between North and South in 1973 should not be allowed to obscure the slow build-up of which it was merely the culmination. One must begin by examining the position of the United States at the centre of the anti-Soviet alliance system and the capitalist world economy. Of these two functions, the first demanded that United States administrations spend largely overseas on the maintenance of military installations and the support of allies. Less directly, the strong military position of the United States in Europe and the Far East reassured American tourists and investors, leading to further dollar outflows. The result was that by the 1960s the USA was running a persistent balance of payments deficit which was covered by the issue of ever larger amounts of dollars.

Foreigners were willing to tolerate this system for a variety of reasons. First, as the leading reserve currency and medium for international trade the US dollar could be regarded as a global public good. Many regarded the US nuclear deterrent in much the same way. For the United States to issue more dollars in order to finance its military role certainly increased the risk that the dollar might one day cease to be convertible, and by doing so it transferred part of the cost of providing both international currency and deterrent to states which were otherwise to some degree free-riders. But because of the usual problem of non-declaration of demand by free-riding consumers of a public good, no one could tell how far the issue of dollars would be tolerated by allies and trading partners of the United States. So long as the Americans continued to run a trade surplus, avert any serious economic recession, and stay clear of prolonged military entanglements, all might be well. But by the late 1960s gross confusion of ideology and interest had brought the United States into an unnecessary, expensive and interminable war in South-East Asia. Tom Paine's dictum that 'forms of government have nothing to do with treaties' had been forgotten in the country of his adoption.[1] At the same time, the massive wave of United States direct foreign investment, a movement subsidized to some degree by the artificially high rate of exchange of the dollar, began to become evident in the form of lost United States exports; in 1970 the US trade account slipped into deficit, giving warning of the incipient obsolescence of the north-eastern industrial cities of the USA. So, in August 1971, came an effective devaluation as the dollar was declared inconvertible.

The story has so far been told in absolute terms, but viewed in relation to her principal allies the decline of the United States during the 1960s was all the more dramatic. Though its immediate intent was strategic, one effect of the post-war dollar outflow had been to boost demand. United States exporters and United States-based multinationals undoubtedly met a good deal of that demand, but some, at least, went to fuel new firms in Europe, Japan and the new industrializing countries, quite independent of US control. By the 1960s some of these had surmounted the initial technological and marketing advantages established by US firms. Much United States investment from the mid-1960s onward was indeed neither positive nor predatory but rather a defensive strategy reluctantly adopted to secure traditional markets under challenge.

So long as the world economy continued to grow, and so long as big United States defence budgets went to support industry, the malaise of the United States economy was concealed, but as soon as growth was checked and weaker producers came under pressure, it became clear that in the United States, almost as much as in the UK, substantial sections of national industrial capacity were no longer competitive with the output of more recently industrialized states such as Japan, South Korea, or Brazil.

The check to growth came almost simultaneously with the dollar crisis and was directly connected with it. By 1970, years of relatively easy credit in the OECD countries had stimulated investment to the point where continued expansion of production was encountering constraints in the supply of labour and raw materials. Strong positions established by labour unions in the long period of relative scarcity of skilled labour now came into play, defending nominal wages, staffing levels, and inefficient units against market pressures. At the same time western growth came hard up against shortages of raw materials. Most primary commodities are inflexible in supply in the short term. New minerals ventures require exploration and considerable investment in infrastructure to come on stream. Many tropical crops take several years from planting to first harvest. The short-term effect was consequently a tightening of primary commodity markets, especially during 1973 and 1974.

Of all the commodities affected by this boom, oil was the most important. The main oil producing states, grouped in the Organization of Petroleum Exporting Countries (OPEC), were able to effect and exploit critical connections between tight conditions in energy markets, diminished US confidence, and third-world demands for reform of the international economic order. For a period of two or three years in the mid-1970s these connections appeared to have made traditional approaches to international affairs obsolete. The moment was to pass, but the stimulus which it gave to the imaginations of students of international affairs would remain, and has had lasting influence on western views of the world.

At the centre of the immediate crisis in 1973 was the continuing war over Palestine. Since its establishment in 1948 the State of Israel had been in permanent conflict with its Arab neighbours: a struggle made all the more intransigent by the presence near Israeli borders of more than half a million Palestinian refugees who had fled the country in 1948 and 1949. The Israelis, many of them effectively refugees from Central and Eastern Europe, had strong ties of kinship and sentiment with influential Jewish communities in the United States, though this was not the only reason why they received support from the United States. Commonly carried on at the diplomatic level or by small-scale terrorist actions, the Arab–Israeli struggle would burst into full-scale war from time to time, and when this happened in October 1973 a new element entered into the conflict. The Organization of Arab Petroluem Exporting Countries (OAPEC) tried to cut off oil supplies to states traditionally sympathetic to the Israeli cause. At the same time the wider OPEC group increased the price of oil very substantially. The price of crude oil was increased from $3.00 to $5.11 a barrel at the Vienna meeting of OPEC in October 1973. Just two months later, in Teheran, a further increase was agreed, to $11.65, making an almost fourfold increase overall.[2]

The Crisis in the Third World

The effects of these events of late 1973 may easily be exaggerated. The Arabs had not sufficient control of oil distribution to use the threat of embargo very precisely. They were to have the satisfaction of seeing France, and later the EEC as a whole, diverge from the US position on the Middle East question, but this was not wholly their own doing. Nor can the movement of the world economy into prolonged recession after 1973 be blamed on OPEC. Besides, a higher oil price would soon have been brought about by market forces had OPEC not acted. In short, the Arabs did no more than take pragmatic advantage of what was for them a happy conjuncture.

This said, the consequences of higher energy costs for North–South relations were manifold and contradictory. In the first place,

DC governments struggling with rising inflation and unemployment were inclined to cut back where they could, and aid budgets suffered accordingly. In addition, higher energy and raw materials costs pushed up the prices of manufactured goods very substantially. These two phenomena, taken together with the hugely increased cost of imported oil, forced those oil-importing LDCs which were considered creditworthy to resort to massive borrowing in order to cover their mounting balance of payments deficits.

The problems faced by the non-oil LDCs could be met only in part and at high cost by the world's bankers. Three other remedies suggested themselves. First of all, the oil exporters might themselves act to eliminate the worst distress caused by their sudden action through aid programmes.

A second tactic was oligopolistic collusion. The success of OPEC in raising petroleum prices appeared to demonstrate the inability of the United States in the Middle East, as in Vietnam, to convert massive destructive capability into usable power. By contrast, it showed the seemingly effective use against the US of economic power. Producers of other raw materials were naturally encouraged by this example and by buoyant demand for their own goods to try to create imitative cartels.

A further, novel, response of the Third World to these events was to bend economic power to diplomatic ends, hitching up the OPEC horse to the UNCTAD pantechnicon. Very much against its will, the US administration was forced in 1974, by the threat of further increases in the price of oil, to give way over the calling of a Conference on International Economic Co-operation (CIEC), the so-called North–South Conference, to discuss a wider range of questions affecting third-world development in the new era of high energy prices. The same threat hung over a great number of negotiations in the three years following the October War. A new round of multilateral trade negotiations (MTN) under the GATT, negotiations to repair or replace the crippled Bretton Woods monetary system, talks aimed at adapting the Yaoundé Convention to a European Community enlarged to include Britain with its retinue of former dependencies, a third United Nations Conference on the Law of the Sea (UNCLOS III), and a further full session of UNCTAD to be held in Nairobi in 1976 all fell under the shadow of Arab oil power.

OPEC Aid

Subsidies to third-world countries especially affected by higher oil prices were an obvious step for the Arab members of OPEC. Their action on prices had not simply been dictated by material considerations, but by their opposition to Israel. It was important for them to maintain as extensive as possible a diplomatic coalition in the UN and elsewhere in order to isolate Israel, and aid offered a relatively simple and inexpensive way of securing cohesion. Saudi Arabia, Libya, and Kuwait had already set out along this path. Their efforts would now be extended and reinforced by the addition of further resources from other OPEC members working through a variety of bilateral and multilateral channels.

Let us straight away put on one side two large groups of transactions which ought not to be considered as concessionary development assistance. First there were the regular amounts, believed to approach $0.5 billion a year by 1973, given to Egypt, Syria, and Jordan to support their war effort, together with additional *ad hoc* amounts for arms purchases. Second there were the very large amounts made available to LDCs through the IMF Oil Facility and the substantial Arab purchases of bonds of the World Bank and the various regional development banks, together running into many billions of dollars. These funds, however, are not to be thought of as amounts transferred. They are more akin to deposits, earning as they do commercial rates of interest.[3]

However, in addition to these substantial sums, the OPEC countries provided very considerable amounts of concessional development assistance. Amongst the institutions created to effect this transfer were the Special Arab Fund for Africa established in 1974, the OPEC Special Fund, and the Arab Bank for Economic Development in Africa. Through these and other agencies OPEC states extended aid worth more than $5 billion a year from 1975 to 1977, only fractionally less than 40 per cent of the total aid provided by the OECD countries during the same period. That such high levels of aid should have been maintained by a group of countries with considerable development problems of their own is partly explained by the large contribution made by the least populous of the oil-rich Arab states. For the 1975–77 period Saudi Arabian aid averaged almost 5 per cent of GNP, while aid from Kuwait and the United Arab Emirates averaged 7.6 and 9.7 per cent respectively. Since these three provided more than three-quarters of OPEC aid, it will be evident that the contribution of the highly absorptive oil-exporters—those populous states whose oil revenues were heavily committed to domestic development programmes—was substantially less. Yet even Nigeria recorded a higher ratio of aid to GNP than Italy, while, by the same measure, Iran, Iraq, and Libya easily outperformed the OECD, implying a very considerable devotion to the Palestinian cause, or to the demand for a new international economic order, or both.[4]

In spite of the very substantial amounts involved, OPEC aid, no less than OECD aid, provoked criticisms from clients before long. The Special Arab Fund for Africa, which aimed specifically to relieve countries suffering from increased oil costs, had disbursed $222 billion by the end of 1978. Grants to Tanzania and Ethiopia, the major recipients, had been sufficient to cover no more than 4 and 8 per cent respectively of the cost of their oil imports over the period 1974-6. Oil-importing LDCs outside the Middle East complained of neglect, pointing out that the bulk of OPEC aid in the mid-1970s went to just two states, Egypt and Syria, both of which were net exporters of petroleum, while a further 25 per cent went to Muslim states such as Mauritania, the Sudan, and Somalia, leaving only 10 per cent of the total amount for non-Islamic countries outside the region. There were also the usual complaints about slow disbursement, and even generously treated states found that OPEC aid did not wholly compensate for higher oil prices. Discontent among non-Arab African states found expression at the Cairo summit conference of Afro-Arab states in March 1977, but was assuaged for the time being by promises of further aid.[5]

Producer Cartels: CIPEC, IBA

If assistance from the OPEC countries helped some non-oil LDCs to balance their external payments, others found, at least in the year or so following the October War, that earnings from their own exports of primary commodities were substantially higher than in the past, so lessening the impact of increased oil prices. 1974 saw the prices of commodities including sugar, olive oil, palm oil, and zinc peak at levels which they would not regain, even in nominal terms, during the remainder of the decade. This firmness, coupled with the example of the OPEC cartel, led to talk of copycat cartels in spite of numerous warnings from economists about the very severe theoretical limits to cartel power.[6]

The *Conseil Intergouvernemental des Pays Exportateurs de Cuivre* (CIPEC) or Intergovernmental Council of Copper-Exporting Countries, established in 1967, was one organization which had tantalizing resemblances to OPEC. Like OPEC, it was solely a producers' club, dominated by a small number of exporting countries—Zambia, Zaïre, Chile, and Peru. Furthermore, political relations between the leading member states were sympathetic. Kenneth Kaunda and

Eduardo Frei, leaders of Zambia and Chile from 1964, are said to have got on well together and to have agreed closely about the means to be adopted to improve the position of exporting countries. In both states, a process of nationalization of the copper industry was under way by the end of the decade, greatly accelerated in Chile by the electoral victory of Salvador Allende at the head of a socialist coalition in 1970. The solidarity that might come from this general agreement on means would be essential if CIPEC were ever to take collective action on prices, because production costs differed substantially from one member state to another, offering lucrative possibilities to free-riders. Peru, though slower to nationalize, was consistent in its economic nationalist attitudes to foreign multinationals first under Belaúnde and subsequently, following the coup of October 1968, under the reformist military regime of General Juan Velasco Alvarado.

CIPEC was plainly a young organization. It was chiefly concerned in the late 1960s with establishing itself and gathering information. Its members did not attempt any collective action at the start of the 1970s as copper prices began to decline. Some commentators have suggested, however, that CIPEC would have acted to defend the price gains of 1973–74 when the market turned down once again in the third quarter of 1974 had it not been for the military coup in Chile.[7] The argument is plausible. In November 1974 CIPEC announced its intention that members should cut their exports to a level 10 per cent below that which had prevailed earlier in the year in an effort to buoy up prices. Further similar directives followed. But preparation of this intervéntion had been poor because, much to their credit, the Zambians had refused to deal with the Chilean *junta* during the months of bloodshed which followed the fall of Allende, and very soon the relatively low-cost Chilean industry began to expand its market share unilaterally, completely ignoring CIPEC directives in 1976 and 1977.[8]

Yet while solidarity might have been a necessary condition for effective CIPEC action after 1974, it surely could not have been sufficient. The founder members of CIPEC together accounted for only 30 per cent of world production of copper ore and 15 per cent of refined copper production in the early 1970s, even including renegade Chile. How could they hope to dictate terms when the chief consumer country, the USA, met only five per cent of its needs from imports?[9] In short CIPEC may have controlled an impressive share of world trade in copper, but not a sufficiently large percentage of world *production* to influence prices; and they dealt in a commodity notoriously substitutable by aluminium and, worse, by secondary copper produced from scrap, which already supplied a third of US requirements by the early 1970s.[10]

On first acquaintance the record of the International Bauxite Association (IBA) might be thought less dismal. Bauxite is used to make aluminium, and the price of this metal continued to rise, though less steeply, during the mid-1970s while others fell back. Moreover the market appeared to be playing into the hands of bauxite-exporting states where governments were anxious to increase the value added to the product within their borders. Largely because of increasing transport costs the major firms were content to bow to pressure from the bauxite states by siting new production of alumina near bauxite sources. The share of LDCs in world alumina production rose from a mere 10 per cent in 1960 to 25 per cent ten years later and 34 per cent in 1975.[11]

Emboldened by these favourable circumstances the more radical of the bauxite-producing states were anxious to press ahead. Guyana began nationalizing the industry in 1971 and joined Jamaica in launching the idea of a producer cartel. Yet the IBA took no collective action on prices until the end of 1977, and even then its declared minimum price was comfortably below the current market level. Instead the Association confined itself to policy co-ordination and the provision of research and technical support, while the North–South battle was waged by the more nationalistic member states acting unilaterally. Jamaica led the way in 1974 by introducing changes in taxation which raised total revenue from $1.77 to $15.08 per ton.[12] The government also began to demand that the state shipping corporation be given a considerable share in carrying bauxite and alumina, as did the Guyanese government.

The result was predictable. The shares in world bauxite production of the more active states fell rapidly and substantially with grave consequences for their economies. The Jamaican line on revenue softened accordingly.[13] Unilateral producer action had been successful in raising revenues and bauxite prices only in the short term. The big aluminium companies could afford to make short-term concessions because rocketing prices for copper and other industrial raw materials for which it could substitute had boosted demand for aluminium in 1973–4 to such an extent that they were able to absorb hugely increased transport, energy, and interest costs, as well as some inflation in the relatively small share of costs accounted for by bauxite itself. In the longer term, they were confident of their ability to elude the Caribbeans. Extensive new sources of bauxite were being opened up in Australia, Guinea, and Brazil. Research into the use of raw materials other than bauxite for aluminium production was well advanced. Finally, the pressures that had led to the location of alumina production near the sources of bauxite did not extend downstream. On the contrary the energy-intensive electrolytic process by which alumina was refined to produce aluminium demanded plentiful and cheap hydroelectric power which the Caribbeans could not supply.[14]

Attempts by producers of iron ore, bananas, coffee, and rubber to defend their export earnings in the face of a general downturn in commodity prices after 1974 fared no better than CIPEC or IBA. The best hope in this field seemed to lie not in independent action by each group of producers, but in a collective approach. By 1976 even the mighty OPEC cartel was looking a lot less formidable than it had done two years before. Recession in the DCs had brought a fall in demand. New non-OPEC sources in Mexico and the North Sea were being brought on stream and there was much talk, over-optimistic as it turned out, about sugar alcohol and other technically innovative substitutes for petroleum. The price of oil had indeed fallen in real terms from the peak of 1974. It remained to be seen whether the all-embracing Integrated Programme for Commodities (IPC) advocated by UNCTAD would prove any more successful than individual commodity cartels.

Private International Lending: Recycling the OPEC Surpluses

The inadequacies of OPEC aid and producer cartels had left a number of oil-importing LDCs in a very difficult position indeed by the mid-1970s. Many lacked alternative energy resources and had effectively locked themselves into dependence on oil, which had been cheap and easily available during their recent phase of rapid growth.

Viewed in aggregate the performance of the non-oil LDCs after 1974 appears relatively good. After a strong start to the decade, growth rates in the DCs had fallen off sharply in the mid- and late-1970s to yield an average rate of growth of GDP for the OECD as a whole of 3.2 per cent per annum for the period 1970–79. This contrasted with a rate of 5.1 per cent per annum achieved in the previous decade. In the Third World, Indian growth continued at the rate established in the 1960s, China accelerated, while the smaller low-income countries fell back from 4.3 to 3.8 per cent per annum, a proportionately smaller decline than that suffered by the DCs. Middle-income LDCs fared better still, falling from 6.1 to 5.5 per cent per annum.[15] This continued growth in the Third World was only possible because the immense balance of payments surpluses accumulated by the OPEC states were recycled to meet the growing deficits of oil-importers and so avert the need for deflation in some cases.

The IMF played only a modest direct role in this process of recycling. As we have already observed, OPEC countries made funds available through the IMF, and an Oil Facility and other special procedures were set up to meet the emergency; but only 3.1 per cent of the financial needs of the LDCs were met from the Fund and other monetary authorities between 1973 and the end of the decade.[16] Moreover, all forms of official lending to the LDCs declined in importance relative to private sources of finance as the international banks increased their commitments. State-guaranteed loans from private financial institutions to the non-oil LDCs rose from 10 to 35 per cent of their medium- and long-term external debt between 1970 and 1979.[17]

Is this to be seen as a liberal parable? The bureaucrats fail to respond flexibly to changed conditions, but markets come good with a minimum of fuss and bother even as politicians meet to discuss suitable reforms to their cumbersome and irrelevant international organizations? LDC statesmen clap their hands in delight at their liberation from the tiresome neo-colonial conditions imposed by the IMF and the World Bank and the tight strings attached to bilateral official aid?

No more than two cheers are in order for the invisible hand. First of all, while it is true that OPEC surpluses were recycled in the 1970s, it should not be forgotten that still larger surpluses could and perhaps should have been recycled, and that a higher level of demand in the world economy as a whole might have permitted growth to continue at 1960s' rates.[18] While the banks handled the mechanics of recycling they were unable to touch the political question of determining the level of effective demand in the world economy. That could be handled only by the major DCs acting unilaterally or, better, in consultation with each other and with the LDCs within the framework of the IMF as attempts to replace the Bretton Woods monetary system went forward.

Even within the macroeconomic constraints established for them, the bankers did a patchy job. A handful of countries received massive sums which brought ratios of debt service to GNP to dangerously high levels in some instances. For the most part the banks loaned to states which were industrializing rapidly—the so-called NICs (Newly Industrializing Countres)—and this category cut right across the divide between exporters and importers of oil to include Mexico, Algeria, Venezuela, and pre-revolution Iran as well as Brazil, South Korea, and Singapore. However since some oil-exporters had substantial funds invested in the Euromarkets, the gross figures are misleading, and it is finally the non-oil NICs, especially Argentina and Brazil, and the more populous oil-exporters, notably Mexico, which emerged as far and away the biggest net borrowers, while the world's poorest states were by and large ignored by the bankers.

This extreme concentration of bank lending holds dangers for the Third World. A serious and prolonged default by Brazil or Mexico could scare off bankers from less profligate Latin American states or NICs for a decade. The reason is not simply that any default would destroy general confidence and dry up the supply of funds (though this is true), but that private financial markets operate a form of conditionality which, though less explicit and politically offensive than that of the IMF, is every bit as important and a good deal more intuitive. Even if they believe it to be a good commercial proposition, bankers will hestitate to make a loan which might reduce confidence in their judgement. That is to say the rationality of the banks' risk assessment procedures may be qualified by the less rational perceptions of depositors and investors. The sensational failure of a country symbolizing oil-based growth or the rising Pacific or some other catch phrase might therefore very easily tar others with the same brush. Sentiment is a powerful force in the marketplace. And a further problem for LDC borrowers is that in a time of increasing protectionism within the DCs the role of major banks in promoting the development of competitive industries in the NICs at some perceived cost to their parent economies could be urged by organized labour and parties of the Left as good reason for tighter regulation or nationalization.[19] At this point the level of the banks' commitment to the LDCs could become a political issue in a struggle which third-world governments could do little to influence. In addition, as the multilateral aid agencies were quick to point out, the apparent lack of conditionality of Eurocurrency loans was an invitation to financial irresponsibility which might land banks and borrowers in difficulties in the long run.[20] The response of the bankers was that recession in the DCs was the main cause of the third-world need to borrow, and that, correspondingly, recovery would provide the new borrowers with ample means to service their debt: a plausible hypothesis, but one as yet untested.[21]

A final reason for rejecting any notion of the 1970s recycling experience as a liberal parable is that in some of the major recipients the rise of bank lending has tightened the hold of the State over the national economy. In Latin America in particular, bank lending has substituted for direct foreign investment by multinational corporations in part. Both sources are private, of course, but

Jeff Frieden describes how, in Mexico, the system of borrowing abroad and then channelling funds through the state-owned *Nacional Financiera* (NAFINSA) 'provides the Mexican government with funds to be disbursed to capital-hungry Mexican industrialists, . . . allows the state to mold the economy, and . . . avoids the political difficulties caused by the multinational corporations. The international banks get their profits,' he continues, 'the Mexican capitalists get their investment capital, and the Mexican government preserves domestic legitimacy by providing funds for economic growth and protection from foreign corporations'.[22]

The Conference on International Economic Co-operation

Variety of financial experience among LDCs in the mid-1970s was only one facet of a general diminution of homogeneity in the Third World precipitated by the recession. Of any single LDC by the middle of the decade one would wish to know whether it was a net importer or exporter of oil; rapidly industrializing or based primarily on agriculture and mining; heavily or lightly indebted, and to whom; a recipient of aid, and whether from the OECD, OPEC, or the Soviet bloc; aligned or non-aligned; restrictive or permissive in attitudes to DFI; centrally-planned or permissive in its domestic economic regime; democratic or authoritarian in constitution. Almost any combination seemed possible, and the range of many of these variables had widened considerably since the 1960s.

The diplomacy to which these circumstances gave rise was of some complexity. Each country decided its position on each issue, within each forum, and for each meeting, not simply with the intention of securing a favourable immediate outcome, but also with an eye to the position in which each possible outcome would place it relative to other participants in future negotiations. As in snooker, it was possible for tactics to develop in one of two ways. In an open game each player in turn would aim at the highest possible score; in a closed game the concern of each would be to ensure that no opportunities for gain were left open to his successor. As in snooker, so in economic diplomacy, the choice of open or closed—aggressive or defensive—tactics was largely determined by the lie of the reds after the break. In the mid-1970s the issue in North–South economic relations which had seemed quite neatly and intelligibly arranged before 1973 broke into a muddled pack in the centre of the table, with several of the high-scoring colours mixed in amongst them: issues such as the law of the sea and nuclear proliferation, which ordinarily had been regarded as discrete from the bundle of trade and development questions which concerned UNCTAD. Experienced players who perhaps had the means to undo this tangle preferred to go for safe shots, clipping a red gently and returning the white to baulk. Debutants, convinced of their ability to execute the single shot that would resolve the balls into an open and easily playable pattern, shot and missed.

But this canny stalemate only developed gradually. Back in 1974 all eyes had been on the power and simplicity of the instrument that was to set things in motion. Oil was dear; oil was scarce; oil was depletable and non-renewable, so that no thought of a decline in its price was to be entertained; oil was powerful. Oil power was to be used to force concessions from the North in a full-scale drive in international organizations for a new international economic order (NIEO).

The fresh offensive opened on the eve of the first OPEC price rise in September 1973. Algerian President, Houari Boumedienne took advantage of his chairmanship of the Organization of Non-Aligned States to stress the intimate connection between international economic institutions and national self-determination. His initiative at the fourth summit conference of the movement in Algiers led to the adoption of a Declaration and Plan of Action for the Establishment of a New International Economic Order (the Declaration of Algiers).[23] The Declaration, which stressed the need to protect the real price of primary commodities, the right of LDCs to expropriate foreign enterprises, and the need for international regulation of multinational firms, was adopted in a Sixth Special Session of the UN General Assembly in May 1974. In December the General Assembly adopted a Charter of Economic Rights and Duties of States, proposed by Mexico, which emphasized sovereignty, autonomy, and non-intervention, the constitutional essentials of a NIEO. The call was picked up and reinforced at a meeting of Commonwealth heads of government in Jamaica in May 1975 and in the Lima meeting of the Non-Aligned Movement in August of the same year, while the Seventh Special Session of the General Assembly forwarded a long list of relevant proposals for consideration at UNCTAD IV, to be held at Nairobi the next year.

Much of this might be thought mere trumpeting, rendered more audible but no more effective by the oil shock. But it coincided with a more radical attempt to break out of the impasse reached in the North–South dialogue through the creation of a new forum, less grandiose than UNCTAD.[24] The key participants in the North–South Conference—properly called the Conference on International Economic Co-operation (CIEC)—were Saudi Arabia, France, Algeria, the EEC, and the USA. It is said to have been the Saudi oil-minister Sheikh Yamani, who first suggested the idea of a conference between the major oil exporters and importers early in 1974. The idea was taken up in October by President Giscard d'Estaing of France, which was the only major consumer state to have stayed outside the International Energy Agency that had been set up under US auspices in the immediate aftermath of the OPEC price rises, when the North Americans still hoped to bully the oil states into reversing their policy. French neutrality in this particular conflict, coupled with historic links between France and Islam and a tradition of French independence from United States foreign policy stances, made Paris a convenient venue. The Americans were persuaded to attend, and a preparatory agenda-setting meeting was arranged for April 1975. The participants were ten in number, with the EEC, the USA, and Japan representing the DCs, Algeria, Iran, Saudi Arabia, and Venezuela, the oil-exporters, and India, Brazil, and Zaïre, the oil-importing LDCs.

Almost at once the USA and Algeria struck extreme attitudes which ensured a breakdown of co-operation. The North Americans wanted the conference to be strictly confined to energy issues. The Algerians, by contrast, were heavily committed to the broader view that all primary commodities should be considered. Only the previous month, as declining non-oil primary commodity prices really began to hurt producers, the Algerians had been prominent in discussions leading to the Solemn Declaration of Algiers, by which OPEC had pledged itself to use the oil weapon to promote the NIEO.

No way was found to bridge the gap between Algeria and the USA and the meeting ended in disarray, but in the Seventh Special Session of the UN General Assembly, not long afterwards, the US position on the commodities issue appeared to soften. Henry Kissinger conceded that 'the methods of development assistance of the 1950s and '60s are no longer adequate', accepted that instability of prices and export earnings harmed both producer and consumer countries, and agreed that the time had come for LDCs to have more say in the administration of international economic institutions.[25] The United States government had finally realized that it could not regain energy self-sufficiency in the short run and that OPEC was not about to collapse.

This easing of United States official attitudes allowed the preparatory group to reconvene successfully in October 1975 and finalize arrangements for a twenty-seven member conference. Australia, Canada, the EEC, Japan, Spain, Sweden, Switzerland, and the USA would face Algeria, Argentina, Brazil, Cameroon, Egypt, India,

Indonesia, Iraq, Iran, Jamaica, Mexico, Nigeria, Pakistan, Peru, Saudi Arabia, Venezuela, Yugoslavia, Zaïre, and Zambia at a first ministerial meeting to be held in December 1975. This meeting duly took place in Paris under the joint chairmanship of Allan MacEachen of Canada and Dr Perez Guerrero of Venezuela, and set up four commissions—on energy, raw materials, development, and finance—each with five DC and ten LDC members under joint DC/LDC chairmanship, which were to start work in February 1976 and report back to a full session of the conference later that year. Disagreement persisted, both on the agenda and the broader purpose of the conference, with the LDCs trying to pin down the DCs and work towards specific agreement on a broad package of measures, while the DCs continued to stress the importance of not treading on the toes of other institutions, such as the IMF, and to uphold the primacy of the energy question within the CIEC. Optimists felt that the CIEC had at least the advantage over UNCTAD of manageable size; pessimists noted that, while it resembled UNCTAD in its rigid group structure, it had not yet evolved efficient ways of aggregating interests within the groups or of signalling the possibilities of compromise between groups. One participant noted that 'the negotiators were largely in the dark regarding each other's possibilities and tolerances'.[26]

These endogenous factors did not augur well, but the fate of the CIEC was finally decided outside the conference hall. During the second half of 1976 the four commissions were to have drawn up proposals for action to be submitted to a final ministerial meeting in December 1976. Timing was vital. OPEC was to meet later the same month to decide price increases. While its more militant members were pressing for a rise of as much as 35 per cent, others favoured something in the region of 10 or 15 per cent. It was strongly hinted that the willingness or unwillingness of the DCs to make concessions in the CIEC could influence the OPEC decision, and the most import-dependent DCs began to prepare the ground for major concessions as the December meetings drew near. West Germany, usually a hard-line opponent of the NIEO, offered to contribute to the controversial Common Fund for Commodities which had figured largely in the year's negotiations with UNCTAD as well as in the CIEC. EEC officials were hinting at a substantial geographical extension of the STABEX system of compensatory finance which they had established for their African, Caribbean, and Pacific (ACP) Associates in 1975.

But at the very last moment the tension evaporated, the ministerial meeting was postponed, and OPEC failed to reach agreement on prices; largely because Saudi Arabia refused to go any further than a 5 per cent rise for the year ahead, well below expectations. Louis Turner has argued that this sheathing of the OPEC sword is to be explained by US diplomatic pressure on Saudi Arabia and the EEC. Towards the end of 1976 the US administration had expressed the view that prospects for a recovery of the world economy were poor, and that any further substantial rise in oil prices would not only hinder economic recovery directly, but might also lead to communist gains in Italy and France which would reduce confidence in the capitalist world economy still further. In addition, it was intimated that President-elect Carter's well-publicized antipathy toward arms sales to Saudi Arabia and Iran could well be hardened into policy by further price rises. At the same time, US officials were hard at work persuading their allies in Western Europe that they had no guarantee whatsoever that concessions in the CIEC would affect OPEC's decision on prices. At a crucial moment a telegram from Secretary of State Kissinger to the US delegation at the CIEC was leaked to the press. It read 'in our view, the connection which some OPEC officials have made between CIEC and OPEC is more rhetorical than actual [and] it is unlikely that OPEC countries view CIEC as a major factor in a decision on oil price increase.'[27] In addition it was argued that nothing binding could in any case be agreed during the White House interregnum between the November electoral victory of Carter and his assumption of power in the New Year, so that the final meeting of the CIEC would have to be postponed until after the OPEC decision on prices.

To the Saudis, a conservative power whose chief foreign policy preoccupation was the achievement of a satisfactory resolution of regional security issues, support for the NIEO was a means to this end, a way of obtaining diplomatic support rather than a campaign to be waged for its own sake. They were therefore extremely responsive to United States arguments which dangled alternative means and possible threats to their ultimate objective before their eyes. There was ample room for a *rapprochement* in which the Saudis would provide moderation on prices within OPEC, moderation *vis-à-vis* Israel in reaching a Middle East settlement, and a bulwark against Soviet influence in the region, while the USA would reciprocate with secure supplies of advanced arms, an enlarged role for the Saudis in the IMF, a safe haven for Arab financial reserves, and pressure on the Israelis to moderate their position.

In short the DCs, stiffened by US cheerleading, had successfully called the OPEC bluff, proving that the more conservative regimes within the Organization were more concerned about a satisfactory

Middle East settlement and the containment of Soviet expansion than about the welfare of non-oil LDCs. The real price of oil was in decline. What is more, the new flexibility of US policy that had surfaced at the Seventh Special Session of the UN General Assembly in 1975 now vanished. It appeared that the most favourable conjuncture which the South had yet encountered had passed away, for the time being at least, and that it was time to review the achievements and experience of the past three years.

Lomé I and the Sugar Protocol

The concrete results of the CIEC were slight. At the final meeting in June 1977 the DCs agreed to contribute to a $1 billion Special Action Programme to help the LDCs most affected by higher oil prices. They agreed in principle to the Common Fund which was being negotiated as part of the Integrated Programme for Commodities (IPC) within UNCTAD, and they pledged themselves to raise the level of development aid in real terms. But these were largely symbolic commitments, and in so far as they called for the disbursement of public funds they could not be carried out without the assent of legislators who were in anything but a generous frame of mind as unemployment and inflation gnawed at their constituencies.

No agreement was reached on energy questions, which had provided the initial reason for the conference. No distinctive or unexpected agreement was reached within this new forum on the problems of trade, debt, and the transfer of technology which were currently dominating discussion within UNCTAD.

The mid-1970s were also a barren period within the GATT. In 1973 a new round of multilateral trade negotiations (MTN) had been launched at a ministerial meeting of the GATT in Tokyo. But the Tokyo Round, as it came to be known, was slow to develop. In the USA the power to negotiate international trade agreements—and indeed treaties of any kind—had always lain with Congress, and the Executive required a specific mandate to engage in GATT talks effectively. This was granted by the US Trade Act of 1974, which set a time limit of five years to negotiations. But by that time, the presidential term was more than half expired and serious negotiation was deferred until the outcome of the 1976 election might be known. So it was not until the late 1970s that the MTN assumed any real importance. However one major international trade agreement of these years outside the GATT did offer grounds for cautious optimism. The first Multifibre Arrangement (MFA) of 1973 which replaced the old cotton LTA certainly went against GATT rules in its extensive use of quotas but was nevertheless welcomed by the NICs since it appeared to be a transitional agreement and ensured growth rates in the region of six per cent each year for their exports of textiles to the DCs, and above all to the EEC, which by 1973 already accounted for 45 per cent of world imports of textile goods. In addition the MFA had been negotiated with greater regard for the wishes of the NICs than had previous agreements and established a new Textile Surveillance Body to settle disputes.[28]

Setting aside the CIEC, then, the stage was held by four distinct sets of negotiations between 1973 and 1976. Relations between the EEC and its ACP associates were being reformed as the UK went into Europe, and this culminated in the Lomé Convention which took effect early in 1975. Central bankers and monetary authorities were busy sifting through the wreckage of the Bretton Woods system in search of answers. They finally reached a truce, though hardly a solution, in Jamaica in 1976. A third United Nations Conference on the Law of the Sea (UNCLOS III) was under way. Finally there was UNCTAD, which attempted at its fourth full session at Nairobi in 1976 to surpass mere prophecy and launch an ambitious campaign to improve the lot of primary producers. Trailing these key negotiations were a series of less prominent confrontations, mostly within the UN system, where issues originally conceived of as non-controversial or as primarily of East–West concern were thrown on the procrustean bed of the North–South dialogue.

The Lomé Convention differed from the Yaoundé Conventions which it replaced in a number of particulars. First of all, the number of associated states covered by the new agreement was greatly increased by the inclusion of many former British dependencies in Africa, the Caribbean, and the Pacific. Secondly, the constitutional arrangements governing the Convention were altered in several ways. Bowing to political reality, the EEC accepted that delegates from the ACP states to the Consultative Assembly need not be parliamentarians, but merely appointees of their respective states. More to the point, the presidency of the Council of Associates, the ministerial body, was now to alternate between the EEC and the ACP, where previously it had remained permanently with the former. A third change was in the amount of multilateral development aid provided by the Community, which was more than tripled from the level of the second Yaoundé Convention to stand at EUA 3,390 for the period 1975-79.[29] A greater role for recipients in the management of aid was assured. Moreover the terms of this assistance were to be easier than in the past, with some softening in the policy of the European Investment Bank, and a grant element of over 80 per cent in aid from the European Development Fund.

But the most important features of the agreement lay in its provisions concerning trade. Here the EEC offered a small improvement in access for goods competing with domestic agricultural production and committed its member states in principle to the extension of the 1971 GSP to cover a wider range of goods as compensation for the non-associable states. In addition, the EEC abandoned its system of reverse preferences which had given great offence to the GATT and UNCTAD and would have been quite unacceptable to Caribbean countries with growing US connections. ACP states no longer had to favour products from the EEC over those from the USA, Japan, or elsewhere. The EEC also made a gesture toward the integration movement in the Third World by altering its rule of origin to treat the ACP states as a single territory. As long as 50 per cent of the value of a manufactured import entering the EEC from any ACP state had been added in one or more of the ACP states, that product would ordinarily be entitled to enter free of duty. Finally there were two initiatives concerning primary commodities. The first of these was an innovative scheme for the stabilization of export earnings (STABEX). STABEX initially covered a list of twelve products including cocoa, coffee, and tea, though it was soon expanded to a wider range of tropical non-mineral primary commodities and to iron ore. So long as any individual ACP country had recently derived more than 7.5 per cent of its export earnings from one of the listed products, it would receive automatic compensation in the form of interest-free loans whenever earnings from its exports of the product in question to the EEC fell by more than 7.5 per cent against the average for the past four years. Nor was this all. For twenty-five of the least-developed ACP countries, and a further eleven considered especially disadvantaged because they were landlocked or islands, the terms of the STABEX scheme were substantially more generous. To qualify, a product had only to account for 2.5 per cent of recent export earnings, and compensation was triggered once earnings fell more than 2.5 per cent below trend. Slightly easier terms were also offered for sisal. STABEX was, in effect, a compensatory finance facility similar to that operated by the IMF, but with a number of important technical modifications and refinements.

The other agreement on primary commodities under the Lomé Convention concerned sugar. The Community of six members, prior to the accession of the UK, Ireland, and Denmark, had been a net exporter of beet sugar, production of which was protected under the Common Agricultural Policy (CAP). Britain, by contrast, had traditionally been a substantial importer and refiner of cane sugar from her Caribbean dependencies and elsewhere, although some beet was grown. With the Commonwealth Sugar Agreement, the International Sugar Agreement, the CAP sugar regulations, and the Yaoundé Convention all due for renegotiation during 1973/4 an unprecedented opportunity existed for sorting out the complex politics of this most political of commodities. At this point the surge in commodity prices transformed the climate of negotiations. Sugar, which had stood as low as $81 per tonne in 1970, had been rising steadily ever since in response to poor 1971 harvests in the USSR and Cuba. By 1973 it had reached $209 per tonne. This doubled in the first quarter of 1974 as the price took off to reach a peak of over $1,000 per tonne in the last three months of the year. Against this background of firm prices and shortage the ACP countries dug in their heels and refused to agree to the remaining provisions of the Lomé Convention unless a satisfactory long-term arrangement for sugar were reached. Accordingly, the EEC agreed in a protocol to the convention to import 1,375,000 tonnes of sugar from the ACP countries at guaranteed prices for seven years. It looked like a major triumph over the hated CAP.[30]

Small wonder then that the Lomé Convention was greeted with widespread enthusiasm as the first fruits of a new era in North–South relations. It showed commodity power in action where it might least have been expected; it made a number of gestures in the direction of more equal status for LDCs in their relations with the North; it placed less emphasis on aid and more on commodity stabilization than past agreements. In all these respects it caught the mood of the moment as negotiations concluded late in 1974.

Debt and Monetary Negotiations

But in the wider world there could be no comfort for the LDCs until the USA, as self-appointed champion of its own eccentric brand of economic liberalism, had given evidence of a change of heart towards the NIEO. Just such a change was detected following the Kissinger speech to the UN of September 1975 and was still evident in the discussions leading up to the Jamaica Agreement of January 1976 on the reform of the IMF.[31]

The evolution of the international monetary system in recent years had been beset by ironies and contradictions. When the SDR was introduced it had seemed as though a way of removing the US dollar from the centre of the stage had been found. The LDCs had not achieved all they wanted, nor were they the guiding force in determining what was achieved, but they could at least regard the reforms of 1969 as a step in the right direction. Yet five years later, on completion of the first issue, SDRs accounted for only four per cent of total world reserves, a figure which would fall thereafter until a second issue began in 1979.[32] In the meantime the dollar continued to constitute roughly four-fifths of world reserves in spite of its inconvertibility and depreciation relative to some other major currencies. Overseas holdings of US dollars as official reserves grew fivefold between 1970 and 1977.[33] All the work of the financial idealists had left international liquidity creation as haphazard and contentious as ever.

This was at least in part because the desperate yet ineffective restrictive measures taken by the US authorities to control their deficits during the later 1960s had ironically served to widen the channels along which liquidity would continue to flood into the world economy during the early years of the next decade.

From as early as 1949, Communist states anxious about financial sanctions in force or threatened against them by the USA had developed the custom of depositing dollar earnings in accounts denominated in dollars but held in Europe, beyond United States' jurisdiction. A market in these offshore dollars developed, and similar markets in the currencies of the major European states also evolved as these were restored to convertibility at the end of the 1950s. Collectively, these funds became known as Eurocurrencies.[34] Up to the mid-1960s most of this business was in the hands of European bankers, but, after the US government introduced ceilings on the rates of interest which domestic banks could pay on time deposits in 1966, a great deal of US money went into Eurodollars and the big US banks promptly dashed to open more European branches to accommodate their clients. Changes in US regulations between 1970 and 1974 halted this highly artificial flight of deposits from the domestic banking system, but not before the attractions of the Euromarkets had become widely known. For many LDCs the marginally higher rates made a switch of some portion of reserves from US or British treasury bills into Eurocurrency deposits very attractive. At the same time, as we have seen, LDCs found in Eurocredits and Eurobonds a route back into the commercial capital market which had been closed to them since the 1930s by tight national restrictions.[35] The irony of it all lay in the fact that of the two chief forms of expression of the *dirigisme* of the professedly liberal US government, the first, an idealistic aspiration to manage the world economy through international organizations, appeared to have been dwarfed, even belittled, by an inadvertent outcome of the more realistically motivated but equally characteristic and ineffective tendency toward tight domestic regulation of Big Money. So by a very roundabout route the Euromarkets had come to provide marginally more palatable ways for the oil-exporters to hold dollars, and, through their lending to the NICs, 'the principal source of new liquidity for the international monetary system'.[36]

This did not prevent discussions on the world monetary system continuing, nor should it have, for while the manner in which international liquidity was created was something which could be left to simmer, the clear breach of its rules created by the move from a fixed to a floating exchange-rate system after the dollar was declared inconvertible in 1971 and the aggravated problems of adjustment which followed 1973 were of pressing and immediate concern to the IMF. The world was operating with a system in which the burden of adjustment to changes in exchange rates was borne by deficit states with non-reserve currencies rather than by states with balance-of-payments surpluses. In addition, there was great disagreement about the rival merits of floating and fixed exchange rates. For the LDCs in particular, each system possessed advantages and disadvantages.[37]

The Jamaica Agreement addressed some of these questions. It legitimized the system of floating rates, accepting a reality it was powerless to alter. More interestingly, it made a direct attempt to improve the position of LDCs while at the same time expanding the function of the SDR. An official dollar price of gold, which had been at the heart of the Bretton Woods system, was dropped. For the IMF itself, gold was to be replaced as unit of account and principal reserve asset by the SDR. The IMF stock of gold would, of course, continue to be valuable, but its value would now be determined in the market, and it would no longer form a necessary element in the international monetary system. Accordingly, one-sixth (about 25 million ounces) was to be sold at auction over the next four years, and the proceeds to be used to provide special balance-of-payments assistance to low-income LDCs. At the same time, an all-round increase in quotas of 25 per cent was agreed.[38] The Second Amendment to the Charter of the IMF, which came into force in April 1978, represented the enactment of the Jamaica Agreement with minor modifications by the Executive Directors of the Fund, and was accompanied by a further general increase in quotas, which further raised the percentage share of the major oil-exporting countries, and hence their voting power.[39]

The United Nations Conference on the Law of the Sea

Though less than global in scope, negotiations between the EEC and its Associates had been unambiguously North–South in character. In monetary negotiations the North would always be inclined to argue that the key to world development lay in the technical problem of finding a satisfactory relationship between major trading currencies, and that explicit negotiation of gimmicks to aid the Third World in the absence of achievement on the larger issue of intra-OECD monetary relations was bound to be fruitless. The same liberal argument that satisfactory pursuit of their interests by the DCs would in all probability produce an outcome to the benefit of the South and that the essential problems were technical ones had passed muster in the late 1950s at UNCLOS I (1958) and UNCLOS II (1960). There, draft conventions drawn up by experts at the UN International Law Commission (ILC) had been pre-circulated for comment and amendment so that the conference delegates met simply to approve polished texts. There was an element of North–South controversy in the proceedings, certainly, since it was mainly the way in which Latin American states had interpreted the Truman proclamation on US sovereignty over the continental shelf when claiming their own 200 mile territorial seas and the threat which this might pose to the major maritime nations of the North which had prompted the conferences in the first place. But there was nothing like the degree of politicization that would characterize UNCLOS III in the 1970s.[40]

As relations between the USA and the USSR improved it was natural that these two major maritime nations should wish to convene a third UN conference to sort out questions left unanswered in 1960. Together with a handful of other major maritime states they were mainly concerned to resolve three kinds of doubt which had overtaken the five conventions agreed at UNCLOS I and UNCLOS II.

The first of these had to do with the rights of innocent passage in territorial waters. In the Geneva Convention on the Territorial Sea and Contiguous Zone of 1958 it had been accepted that the sovereignty of a state extended to a belt of sea beyond its coasts, but that this sovereignty was limited by a number of rights in international law of which the right of innocent passage, and, in particular, the right of vessels to pass through international straits, was one of the most important. Over the years, a number of states had questioned whether the passage of a vessel should be regarded as innocent until proven guilty or guilty until proven innocent. Some felt that innocent passage should not be accorded to vessels such as oil tankers, where a strong risk of pollution existed, or to warships, whose intentions could never be regarded as entirely innocent. The major maritime states naturally dissented and wished to secure a clarification of the legal position.

A second major difficulty, arising from the same convention and having wide implications, was the vagueness which persisted concerning the extent of the territorial sea beyond the baselines or coasts of each state. The 1958 convention had dealt with the rather more limited powers which coastal states might exercise in a zone 'contiguous to its territorial sea but limited to a distance of 12 miles from its baselines'.[41] This seemed to imply that the territorial sea must extend no more than twelve miles, and indeed at UNCLOS II the maritime powers had tried and failed to get explicit agreement on a six-mile band of territorial sea with a further six-mile contiguous zone in which each coastal state would have exclusive fishing rights as well as the right to enforce customs and immigration regulations, but which would otherwise be deemed part of the high seas. The ambiguity was exploited by a number of states, mainly Latin American, which continued to maintain their claims to 200-mile territorial seas.

The third problem related to the continental shelf. In 1945 the USA had claimed limited sovereignty over its continental shelf, pleading the need to manage migratory fish species and to guard against submarines. A Convention agreed at UNCLOS I made clear that the rights exercised by the USA and other states on the continental shelf and its subsoil fell well short of sovereignty, amounting essentially to a right to explore and to expropriate seabed resources, but not a title to undiscovered resources. In addition the Convention defined the continental shelf, but it did so in an unsatisfactory way, allowing a coastal state in effect to count as continental shelf any area contiguous to its coasts up to the point where depth made exploitation of natural resources impossible. This meant that the extent of a state's legally defined continental shelf became a function of the technological expertise of its mining engineers and that, in principle, the ocean floor lay open to the first country or firm to overcome the immense practical problems posed by deep water. This had been of limited practical concern so long as offshore technology remained relatively primitive, but threatened to give rise to disputes if, as seemed likely, commercially viable techniques for exploiting the reputedly vast wealth of seabed mineral resources were developed.

But if maritime powers had hoped for a further neat exercise in law-making with gentlemanly disagreements resolved by the officials before the plenipotentiaries were wheeled in to sign a new convention at a brief and amicable UNCLOS III, then they were to be sorely disappointed, and guilty too of a myopic failure to observe the gradual infiltration of third-world ideological considerations and Group of 77 influence into this forum. In the early years of independence a great many new states had neglected to join the UN Seabed Committee, feeling no doubt that this was a technical body of real interest only to a relatively small number of coastal states with the capability to engage in commercially or militarily significant marine activity. But after 1968, as proposals for a third UNCLOS began to be voiced, new members flocked in. Moreover the new participants raised new issues. In the first place, they included a great many relatively weak coastal states that shared the apprehension of Australia, Canada, and the Latin Americans over the long-term implications of expanding Japanese, Soviet, and US marine exploration and research programmes and wanted a general strengthening of property rights in order to be quite sure of their just deserts once offshore and deep seabed minerals exploration began in earnest. Secondly, there were those states which were either landlocked or had such short coastlines relative to their area or population that they could reasonably be considered disadvantaged. These land-locked and geographically disadvantaged states (LLGDS) viewed the appropriation and exploitation of marine resources by coastal states alone as arbitrary and unjust and were prepared to use their right to participate in and ability to block UN negotiations as a weapon to secure some crumbs from the table. The LLGDS were mobilized by one of the DCs, Austria, but included a good number of third-world states, many of them very poor indeed, which shared a more general interest with coastal LDCs in attempting to achieve a deep seabed mining regime which would transfer resources from North to South. Finally, there were those copper, nickel, and manganese producing countries—developed as well as under-developed—which looked to receive compensation for or control of expanding seabed production in order to protect their export earnings.[42]

These developments ensured that UNCLOS III, summoned by the UN General Assembly in 1973, would be contentious, prolonged, and wide-ranging, with a strong tendency towards North–South division in some of its crucial negotiating groups. They also made it probable that the major maritime states would have to make substantial concessions to LDCs in order to get the legal clarifications they needed before they could safely proceed to apply new technologies in the oceans. It was not long, therefore, until UNCLOS III began to attract the attention of commentators on international organization and North–South relations. From 1974 onwards it became almost a standing organization with frequent plenary sessions involving as many as 140 states and 1,100 delegates. It was distinguished not only by the sheer scale of its operations but by a determination to reach all decisions by consensus and avoid formal voting until the negotiations were at an end. If successful it would surely attract imitators. Failure, on the other hand, could infect and embitter North–South debate in other forums both within the UN family and elsewhere.[43]

Discussion took place in three main committees. The first was concerned with the regime for the deep seabed. The second was to debate jurisdictional questions concerning the definition of the continental shelf, and the notion of a 200-mile Exclusive Economic Zone (EEZ), which had by 1974 replaced the old Latin American claim of a 200-mile territorial sea as the rallying call of the vast majority of coastal states. The third committee was to examine questions concerning marine scientific research and pollution.

Disagreements arose in all three committees. Flag-of-convenience states were less enthusiastic than others about changes in the law which would make the enforcement of anti-pollution regulations by coastal states easier and more effective. In the second committee the major maritime states were predictably reluctant to assent to a regime which would permit massive proliferation of regulation in coastal and near-coastal waters. Yet although these and other divisions persisted up to 1976 it was differences of view on the deep seabed question in the first committee that appeared the most intractable of all. Accordingly the early days of the sixth session of UNCLOS III were devoted to breaking this deadlock, and resulted in the incorporation of a compromise formula drafted by Paul Engo, chairman of the first committee, into the informal composite negotiating text (ICNT) on which the final negotiating sessions were to be based.

The Engo text envisaged an International Seabed Authority (ISA) that would exercise a monopoly over deep seabed resources, which were to be regarded as the common heritage of mankind. The ISA would allow access to companies or consortia with the skills needed to exploit these resources only on terms which included some element of assistance to LDCs, either in the form of transfer of technology or contributions to revenue. The ISA would be governed by an assembly, voting on a one-state-one-vote principle and requiring a two-thirds majority for most decisions. Production controls demanded by Chile, Zaïre, Canada, and other mineral producers were included, and in addition the ISA was to participate in appropriate international commodity agreements.

The ICNT did not represent an agreement so much as a series of artists' impressions of the sorts of compromises which might eventually be reached by the Conference. It was essentially designed to permit negotiations to proceed along more specific and constrained paths. However, publication of the ICNT in 1977 had almost the opposite effect from that intended, as the United States government, taking the greatest exception to the Engo text on the deep seabed regime, announced its intention to embark upon a review of its participation in UNCLOS III, apparently threatening to jettison the work of three years.

The United Nations Conference on Trade and Development

During the early months of 1976, however, this reversal at UNCLOS and United States subversion of the CIEC still lay in the future. It remained to be seen whether the modest progress claimed by the South at the IMF talks in Jamaica in January and the changed relationship with the EEC would spill over into what still remained the central forum of the North–South debate, UNCTAD.

UNCTAD had been far from idle since the disappointing Santiago meeting in 1972. In its work on shipping and multinational corporations it had sponsored considerable research and gone some way towards securing international agreement to regulatory codes of conduct. International shipping had long been dominated by northern firms. About a third of the world's merchant fleet is now registered in US client states in the Third World such as Liberia and Panama which offer flags of convenience. Here owners may avoid the high costs of compliance with DC labour rates, safety regulations, and bureaucratic procedures. But most of these vessels are owned in the major maritime states of the North; indeed it is estimated that US firms own 21 per cent and EEC firms 27 per cent of the world merchant fleet.[44]

This has meant that the international trade of third-world states has been almost exclusively carried in foreign ships and has encouraged sensitivity to pricing policies and the quality of service provided, and to the drain on foreign-exchange resources and loss of domestic employment opportunities entailed by imported shipping services. At times this sensitivity has spilled over into nationalism as individual states have reserved some part of their trade for national fleets. The USA has long reserved to its own ships its coastal trade, including trade between Hawaii and Alaska and the mainland, and has additionally insisted that half of all aid cargoes be carried in ships sailing under the US flag. Many Latin American states have also established national fleets behind protective regulations of this sort.[45]

In discussions within the Group of 77 and UNCTAD during the 1960s, this protectionist sentiment became generalized. It was argued that third-world states ought to be able to reserve some part of their traffic to national fleets in order to be able to ensure supply and influence the prices of their exports, to encourage their ship-building industries, to assist their foreign exchange earnings, and for reasons of prestige. These ambitions took shape in the demand for a legally binding code of conduct including a cargo-sharing formula to govern liner conferences. Liners provide regular scheduled ship-ping services and account for only a fifth of world cargo, the remainder of which is moved in bulk carriers, such as oil tankers, which often belong to large vertically-integrated extractive enter-prises.[46] Conferences are the regular collusive arrangements through which liner operators have attempted over more than a century to control price competition. The most contentious part of the UN Code of Conduct drafted in 1974 was the suggestion that the liner cargo passing between any two states be divided in such a way that 40 per cent was carried in the ships of each state, while only the remaining 20 per cent would still be available for third parties, or cross-traders, of which the most vulnerable are the UK, Denmark, and Greece.

In spite of opposition from the major maritime states, the UNCTAD Code was approved in 1974 and the Group of 77, em-boldened by this, introduced the idea of a similar code to cover bulk shipping on to the agenda for UNCTAD V; but towards the end of 1974 the prospect of the Liner Code coming into force receded as the EEC decided that individual member states could not, as France and West Germany had, ratify such an agreement unilaterally. Ratification must be by the Community as a whole and could only follow prolonged internal wrangling.[47]

Another major concern of UNCTAD from its inception had been the activities of multinational corporations. The biggest of these produced goods to a value exceeding the GNP of many states, employed tens of thousands of workers, and could frustrate the policies of national governments. Though the bulk of their sales and activities took place in the western DCs in which most were based, where they had given rise to considerable concern in France, Canada, and elsewhere, it was in the Third World that the strongest complaints had been voiced.[48] This was partly because the activities of individual firms often loomed large within small third-world economies, partly because third-world activities more often involved politically sensitive soliciting of concessions or privileges from states or the exercise of monopoly.[49] Public utilities, insurance, banking, civil engineering, plantations, and mining have typically offered opportunities to fragile third-world regimes in search of whipping-boys, and US firms in particular have often shown an astonishing lack of political sensitivity and aplomb in these circumstances.[50]

Individual states had for many years legislated to control MNCs within their boundaries, but many governments, not just in the Third World, had increasingly come to feel that they were being outflanked by the corporations, which appeared able to divert resources from one subsidiary company to another across national boundaries, to make states bid against one another for fresh invest-ment, and to use the threat of closing down operations as a means of influencing the policies of employment-sensitive governments and curbing the demands of labour. There seemed therefore to be a prima-facie case for harmonizing national regimes at least, and possibly for agreeing international standards.

This drive towards international legislation was not confined to UNCTAD. When the Group of Eminent Persons commissioned by ECOSOC in 1972 to study the MNC question reported in 1974 it recommended the creation of a Commission on Transnational Cor-porations (CTN) and a Centre on Transnational Corporations (CTC), which together would supervise an Information and Research Centre (IRC). One aim of the CTN was to be the elaboration of a code of conduct for transnational corporations (TNCs) (a term preferred in the UN to the more common 'multinational corporation' or 'multi-national enterprise' (MNE)), and it is indicative both of the wide-spread interest in problems arising from direct foreign investment (DFI) and the tangled and overlapping network of the UN that CTN meetings to discuss such a code were attended by representatives from UNCTAD, the International Labour Office (ILO), the Food and Agriculture Organizations (FAO), the IMF, the United Nations Industrial Development Organization (UNIDO), and the United Nations Education and Scientific Commission (UNESCO).[51]

By its Lima meeting of March 1976, the CTN had clearly decided that the code of conduct should be its main objective. But this would be in essence the overarching embellishment of a number of more specific and detailed codes negotiated elsewhere: the one relating to labour questions in the ILO, and those covering restrictive business practices and the transfer of technology in UNCTAD. However, although work on these codes had been initiated by 1976, as, too, had a closely related revision of international patent law conducted by the World Intellectual Property Organization, it would clearly be some time before anything of substance emerged. In the meantime, UNCTAD IV did at least move the process on a step by securing agreement to hold a negotiating conference on the transfer of technology code.

Yet for all this activity on shipping and MNCs, the principal concern of the UNCTAD secretariat since 1974, when the General Assembly had commissioned it to prepare 'an overall integrated programme . . . for a comprehensive range of commodities of export interest to developing countries', had been primary commodities. A series of ICAs negotiated within the UNCTAD framework was envisaged to cover cocoa, coffee, tea, sugar, tin, rubber, cotton, jute, hard fibres, and copper. Stability of each of these ten core commodities would be ensured by a buffer stock, which would buy when prices were weak and sell when they recovered. This kind of agreement had met with very limited success in the past, and the novel feature of the UNCTAD programme was that a common fund was to link the ICAs, enabling the temporary weakness of any one to be compensated for by the strength of the others and offering the possibility of some intervention in eight other commodities including bananas, vegetable oils, meat, timber, iron ore, bauxite, manganese, and phosphates, which for one reason or another were felt to be more problematic than the core commodities. In addition to the ICAs and the Common Fund, stability was to be ensured by long-term supply contacts, compensatory finance arrangements on the lines of the IMF, CFF or STABEX to cover variations in export earnings, and policies to increase the value added to commodities within producer states and to diversify production.

By the time UNCTAD met in Nairobi in 1976, the prices of many primary commodities were well down from their 1974-5 peaks, but the mood of the previous two years had not yet entirely evaporated. DC delegates were inclined to assume, in spite of UNCTAD denials, that the aim of the IPC was not simply to stabilize commodity prices, but to stabilize them at levels higher than they would otherwise have averaged.[52] Western economists were quick to point out that stable prices would by no means assure stable earnings, that neither stable prices nor stable earnings would guarantee more rapid growth, and that the benefit of such a scheme would in all probability accrue mainly to a relatively small group of high income LDCs and DCs.

Such discussion was made very difficult by the fact that, at this stage, there was no detailed proposal on the table. What the UNCTAD secretariat wanted, and finally achieved, was an agreement in principle to start negotiating a Common Fund, the details of which would then be hammered out in committee. In the meantime, their principal concern was to preserve the unity of the Group of 77 and conclude the plenary session of the Conference in a way that could credibly be presented to the world as a success and would confirm UNCTAD's central role in world commodity negotiations. There was, in short, a strong institutional need within UNCTAD for agreement on this issue, however empty of content. Members of the Group of 77 for their part either dismissed reports which suggested that many of them might actually lose by such a scheme as DC propaganda or else accepted them but reasoned that it was not sensible to break ranks with the pack and lose its collective support on other issues in order to oppose a scheme which would surely eventually be hobbled by the DCs without their help.[53] As for the DCs, they disagreed, with some of the EEC states tending to favour the IPC, while Britain and West Germany were pretty much opposed to it, the latter attempting to use the concurrent renegotiation of the Lomé Convention to sow discord on this very issue with the Group of 77. The USA, which was emphatically against the Common Fund idea, was able to make some headway with an alternative approach stressing increased investment through an International Resources Bank (IRB) with an initial capital of $1 billion, security of supply, greater scope for private enterprise, and additional compensatory finance of $2.5 billion a year or more through a new Development Security Facility. But the IRB was narrowly defeated at Nairobi, and was interpreted by the Group of 77 as a divisive and therefore hostile device dreamed up by the Americans to tempt those low-income LDCs with serious debt problems to defect.

The result was a deadlock only broken at the last moment by a small contact group in the upper regions of the Nairobi Hilton which came up with an exquisitely ambiguous formula whereby the Secretary General was to be requested to call a negotiating conference and various preparatory meetings by March 1977 to discuss a common fund—not, it should be stressed, any particular common fund, let alone *the* Common Fund.[54] UNCTAD IV also agreed to hold conferences on debt relief as well as on the transfer of technology in the near future.

Just how meagre these achievements were would only gradually become apparent over the next three years. At the conclusion of UNCTAD IV the CIEC was still in session, the oil threat still to be feared, and the recession assumed temporary, though US policy was already hardening after its brief conciliatory phase in 1975 and early 1976. In Iran the Shah still ruled. No one anticipated a further round of increases in oil prices of the same order as those of 1973–4.

Notes

1. The remark was made apropos of Paine's forecast that the republican USA and monarchist France would remain allies on the basis of interest. It is quoted by Henry Collins in his introduction to Tom Paine, *Rights of Man* (Pelican edition, Harmondsworth, Penguin, 1969), p. 26.
2. Lars Anell and Birgitta Nygren, *The Developing Countries and the World Economic Order* (London, Frances Pinter, 1980), p. 102.
3. Maurice J. Williams, 'The Aid Problems of the OPEC Countries', *Foreign Affairs*, 54 (1976), pp. 309, 315.
4. *World Development Report, 1981* (New York, IBRD, 1981), Table 16, pp. 164–5.
5. Williams, op. cit., Ian Seymour, *OPEC: Instrument of Change* (London, Macmillan, 1980), pp. 236–66; I. Shihata and Robert Mabro, 'The OPEC Aid Record', *World Development*, 7 (1979), 161–73; Paul Hallwood and Stuart Sinclair, *Oil, Debt, and Development: OPEC in the Third World* (London, Allen & Unwin, 1981), pp. 94–128.
6. See Paul Streeten, 'The Dynamics of the New Poor Power', in G. K. Helleiner, ed., *A World Divided: the less developed countries in the international economy* (Cambridge, Cambridge University Press, 1976), pp. 77–88.
7. Stephen A. Zorn, 'Producers' Associations and Commodity Markets: the case of CIPEC', in F. Gerard Adams and Sonia A. Klein, eds, *Stabilizing World Commodity Markets* (Lexington, Mass., Lexington Books, 1978), p. 227, argues that 'the market situation was at its most favourable for producer action [in 1973/4], since the countries' foreign exchange earnings were at relatively high levels and the strong demand in industrial countries made a pass through of raw materials costs to ultimate consumers easier than it would have been in a period of stagnating demand'.
8. Carmine Nappi, *Commodity Market Controls: a historical review* (Lexington, Mass., Lexington Books, 1979), p. 114; Stephen A. Zorn, op. cit., pp. 228–9.
9. Nappi, op. cit., p. 108.
10. Ibid.
11. Nappi, op. cit., p. 121.
12. Ibid.
13. Albert Fishlow, 'A New International Economic Order: What Kind?' in Albert Fishlow, *et al.*, *Rich and Poor Nations in the World Economy* (New York, McGraw-Hill, 1978), p. 34.
14. Nappi, op. cit., p. 136.
15. *World Development Report, 1981*, Table 2, pp. 136–7.
16. Frances Stewart and Arjun Sengupta, *International Financial Cooperation: a Framework for Change* (London and Boulder, Col., Frances Pinter, 1982), p. 15.
17. Ibid., p. 15, Table 2.4.
18. 'A less deflationary stance [by DCs after 1973] giving greater emphasis to making new investments so as to adjust economic structures to the new international environment, would have bolstered world demand for LDC exports, limited the size of OPEC surpluses, and thus reduced the counterpart deficits in the Third World'. Tony Killick, 'Eurocurrency Market Recycling of OPEC Surpluses to Developing Countries: fact or myth?', in

C. Stevens, ed., *EEC and the Third World* (London, Hodder & Stoughton, 1981), p. 95.

19. See M. Stefan Mendelsohn, *Money on the Move: the Modern International Capital Market* (New York, McGraw-Hill, 1980), Chapter 10.
20. See, for example, the Jeremiads quoted by Carlos Díaz-Alejandro in his essay, 'The Post-1971 International Financial System and the Less Developed Countries', in Helleiner, ed., *A World Divided*, pp. 191-2.
21. This view is taken in Harold van B. Cleveland and Wilt B. Brittain, 'Are the LDCs in over their Heads?', *Foreign Affairs*, 55 (1977), 732-50. In the absence of recovery in the OECD countries, these thoughts, offered as comfort, become alarm bells.
22. Jeff Frieden, 'Third World Indebted Industrialization: international finance and state capitalism in Mexico, Brazil, Algeria, and South Korea', *International Organization*, 35 (1981), p. 418. See also Peter Evans, *Dependent Development: the Alliance of Multinational, State, and Local Capital in Brazil* (Princeton, NJ, Princeton University Press, 1979).
23. Published collections of documents are numerous. See Alfred G. Moss and H. N. M. Winton, eds, *A New International Economic Order: selected documents, 1954-1975* (New York, UNITAR, 1976); Karl K. Sauvant and Hajo Hasenplug, eds, *The New International Economic Order: Confrontation or Cooperation between North and South?* (Boulder, Col., Westview, 1977); Karl P. Sauvant, *Changing Priorities on the International Agenda: the New International Economic Order* (New York, Pergamon, 1981). Ervin Laszlo, Robert Baker Jr, Elliott Eisenberg, and Venkata Raman, *The Objectives of a New International Economic Order* (New York, Pergamon, 1978, for UNITAR) uses short quotations from key documents to outline the demands comprising the NIEO and the positions of major states and groups on each issue.
24. This account relies chiefly upon Louis Turner, 'Oil and the North–South Dialogue', *The World Today*, February 1977, 52-61, and the same author's 'The North–South Dialogue', *The World Today*, February 1976, 81-3; Louis Turner and Audrey Parry, 'The Next Steps in Energy Cooperation', *The World Today*, March 1978; Sam Younger, 'Ideology and Pragmatism in Algerian Foreign Policy', *The World Today*, March 1978, 112-14; Johangir Amuzegar, 'A Requiem for the North–South Conference', *Foreign Affairs*, 56 (1977), 136-59.
25. Henry Kissinger, 'Global Consensus and Economic Development', *US Department of State Bulletin*, 73 (22 September 1975), 427-40, quoted in David L. McNicol, *Commodity Agreements and Price Stabilization* (Lexington, Mass., Lexington Books, 1978), pp. 103-5.
26. Amuzegar, 'A Requiem for the North–South Conference', p. 153.
27. *Sunday Times*, 12 December 1976, quoted in Robert L. Rothstein, *Global Bargaining: UNCTAD and the quest for a New International Economic Order* (Princeton, NJ, Princeton University Press, 1979), p. 47, n. 16.
28. Chris Farrands, 'The Political Economy of the Multifibre Arrangement', in Christopher Stevens, ed., *EEC and the Third World: a survey—II. Hunger in the World* (London, Hodder & Stoughton, 1982), pp. 91-3.
29. The European Unit of Account (EUA) was originally equal to the US dollar.
30. Ian Smith, 'Sugar Markets in Disarray', *Journal of World Trade Law*, 9 (1975), 41-62; Simon Z. Young, *Terms of Entry* (London, Heinemann, 1973), pp. 154-66.

31. The Jamaica Agreement is seen as the principal fruit of a more conciliatory phase in its policy toward the Third World following initial US intransigence on the NIEO by Albert Fishlow in his 'Introduction' to Fishlow *et al.*, *Rich and Poor Nations in the World Economy*, p. 12. The account which follows is largely based on Gerald M. Meier, 'The "Jamaica Agreement", International Monetary Reform, and the Developing Countries', *Journal of International Law and Economics*, 11 (1977), 67–89; Duncan Cameron, 'The Reform of International Money', *International Journal*, 34 (1978–9), 90–109; and Duncan Cameron, 'Special Drawing Rights', *International Journal*, 36 (1981), 713–31.
32. Cameron, 'Special Drawing Rights', pp. 722–3.
33. Cameron, 'The Reform of International Money', p. 96.
34. The clearest account I know of the evolution of Euromarkets is Mendelsohn, *Money on the Move*, Part 1.
35. These are outlined in Carlos F. Díaz-Alejandro, 'The Post-1971 International Financial System and the Less Developed Countries', in Helleiner, ed., *A World Divided*, p. 195.
36. Cameron, 'Special Drawing Rights', p. 720.
37. Díaz-Alejandro, op. cit., pp. 177–88.
38. Gerald M. Meier, 'The "Jamaica Agreement", International monetary Reform and the Developing Countries', *Journal of International Law and Economics*, 2 (1977), 67–89.
39. George C. Abbot, 'Recent Developments in the International Monetary System and their implications for International Economic Relations', *Journal of Economic Studies*, 6 (1979), pp. 133 and 143–6.
40. P. W. Birnie, 'The Law of the Sea before and after UNCLOS I and UNCLOS II', in R. P. Barston and P. Birnie, eds, *The Maritime Dimension* (London, Allen & Unwin, 1980), 8–26.
41. Ibid., p. 16.
42. Edward Miles, 'The Dynamics of Global Ocean Politics', in Douglas M. Johnston, ed., *Marine Policy and the Coastal Community: the Impact of the Law of the Sea* (London, Croom Helm, 1976), 147–81.
43. R. P. Barston, 'The Law of the Sea Conference: the Search for New Regimes', in Barston and Birnie, eds, *The Maritime Dimension*, pp. 154–68.
44. Ronald Hope, 'The Political Economy of Marine Transportation', in Johnston, ed., *Marine Policy and the Coastal Community*, pp. 103–43.
45. Christopher Hayman, 'International Shipping', in Barston and Birnie, eds, *The Maritime Dimension*, p. 131.
46. Stephen C. Neff, 'The UN Code of Conduct for Liner Conferences', *Journal of World Trade Law*, 14 (1980), p. 399. For background see Susan Strange, 'Who Runs World Shipping?', *International Affairs*, 52 (1976), 346–67, and on the conference system and early Latin American reactions to it see Robert Greenhill, 'Shipping, 1850–1914', in D. C. M. Platt, ed., *Business Imperialism, 1840–1930: an Inquiry Based on British Experience in Latin America* (Oxford, Clarendon Press, 1977), pp. 119–55.
47. Hayman, 'International Shipping', p. 134.
48. On France and Canada respectively see Jean-Jacques Servan-Schreiber, *The American Challenge* (Harmondsworth, Penguin, 1970 (first edition, 1968)) and Kari Levitt, *The Silent Surrender: the Multinational Corporation in Canada* (Toronto, Liveright Publishing Corp., 1970). A useful general survey is to be found in Raymond Vernon, *Storm over the Multinationals: the Real Issues* (London, Macmillan, 1977).

49. On the historical evolution of this state of affairs, see C. A. Jones, ' "Business Imperialism" and Argentina, 1875–1900: a Theoretical Note', *Journal of Latin American Studies,* 12 (1980), 437–44.
50. Something of the interplay of local politics and MNC behaviour may be gleaned from the essays in Platt, ed., *Business Imperialism, 1840–1930*. My singling out of US firms is based on observations too numerous to cite here. To those who regard it as mere prejudice I would reply only that it is a widely-held view, and therefore of some political consequence, referring them to data on the subject of third-world perceptions of the relative merits of US, European, and Japanese-owned MNCs in Anant R. Negandhi, *Quest for Survival and Growth: a Comparative Study of American, European, and Japanese Multinationals* (New York, Praeger, 1979).
51. Werner J. Feld, *Multinational Corporations and UN Politics: the quest for codes of conduct* (New York, Pergamon, 1980), pp. 35 *et seq.*
52. 'McNichol's suspicion that "stable" prices were a euphemism for "higher" prices was widely shared' (Robert L. Rothstein, *Global Bargaining*, p. 75, citing McNicol, *Commodity Agreements and the New International Economic Order*, p. 27).
53. Rothstein, *Global Bargaining*, p. 119, attributes this line of reasoning to a few, very sophisticated states.
54. Ibid., p. 133.

4 THE DIALOGUE STALLED

The End of Détente

One effect of the ignominious withdrawal of United States forces from South-East Asia had been to persuade many people that military force was now so expensive and clumsy an instrument of foreign policy that even the world's wealthiest state was not able to employ it adroitly. The oil embargo of 1973 and the subsequent drift of EEC and Japanese policy on the Arab–Israeli question seemed to illustrate neatly the chief corollary of this thesis, which was that economic suasion could bring the rich to their knees in an inter-dependent world. But these events on the post-colonial periphery would not have had anything like so strong an impact had they not taken place in what was already established as a period of markedly reduced hostility between the major powers.

From the end of the 1960s a comfortable feeling had begun to settle upon the industrialized world. The Soviet Union had at last attained a very rough weapons parity with the USA, and this appeared to make nuclear war less likely since the strength of each was believed effectively to deter attack by the other. Peace movements languished. World leaders began to talk across barriers which had divided them for twenty years. President Nixon visited Moscow and Peking. Talks between the USA and the Soviet Union led to the signature of a strategic arms limitation treaty (SALT I) and to numerous com-mercial and cultural agreements. Many longstanding disputes were settled in Europe, where the Russians at last signed a treaty with West Germany and a European Security Conference at Helsinki in 1975 brought mutual commitment to current European frontiers and minimal guarantees on human rights.

Against this backdrop of reduced tension, third-world states had briefly succeeded in applying leverage to the developed capitalist states of the North. Even when this temporary advantage dis-appeared, both sides had been happy enough to continue their dialogue in the United Nations and elsewhere and to make much of their modest achievements, because there was no clear advantage to be gained by either side from adopting hostile and inflexible public postures, however slight might be the scope for private negotiations and substantive concessions. But from the middle of the decade events were tending more and more to undermine this frail North–South accommodation.

Following the *coup d'état* of 1974 in Portugal, the African dependencies of this most obdurate of the colonial powers moved unsteadily towards independence. The USA, South Africa, and the Soviet Union had taken sides in the struggle and were all supplying arms by the end of 1974. All-out civil war commenced the following March, but events took a new turn in the closing months of the year when Cuban troops intervened decisively to support the Soviet-backed MPLA against South African forces attacking from the South alongside rival FNLA and UNITA troops.

Further African embarrassments for the USA soon followed. The USSR and Cuba again dictated events when Somalia attacked neighbouring Ethiopia in July 1977. Formerly on good terms with both states, the Soviet Union came off the fence to oppose the Somali invasion, occasioning an Ethiopian victory in March 1978.[1] The French, too, were much in evidence in Africa, intervening at the request of President Mobutu of Zaïre and Hassan of Morocco to provide air support against Angola-based forces opposed to Mobutu in 1977 and 1978, making air-strikes in support of the Moroccan and Mauritanian governments against Polisario rebels in the Sahara later the same year, and ousting the self-styled Emperor Bokassa from Central Africa in 1979.[2]

These events would be interpreted in Washington as, at the very least, evidence of a lack of United States grip on events, and, at worst, of Soviet bad faith and growing European autonomy; yet they might be dismissed as peripheral so long as major third-world conflicts in the Middle East and South-East Asia were proving more malleable and relations with other great powers were relatively stable. Broadly speaking, this continued to be the case until 1979, at which point the whole edifice of *détente*, fatally undermined by the events of the past five years, came tumbling down.

Ever since the 1973 War, Egypt had been moving steadily towards a settlement with Israel. Control over the Suez Canal had been recovered by 1975. In September of that year an Israeli–Egyptian agreement on Sinai led to the temporary ostracism of Egypt by the PLO and the Syrians, who considered the Egyptian move subversive of the wider Arab front against Israel. But in November 1977 Sadat pushed the negotiating process a step further by visiting Jerusalem, opening up a path which led by way of the Camp David Agreements of September 1978 to a peace treaty between Egypt and Israel in March 1979.

Egyptian policy was criticized publicly by other Arab states. Yet the more conservative powers that formed the financial backbone of the alliance were generally anxious to reach a compromise which would secure for the Palestinians something short of an independent, revolutionary republic. Fully aware of this, the Palestine Liberation Organization (PLO) leadership itself took an increasingly moderate line on the precise constitutional forms that a Palestinian homeland should take. This promising convergence was eventually to founder in 1982 when the inveterate opportunism of PLO units in Lebanon and elsewhere finally provided an intransigent and contemptuous Israeli government with rationalization for a major military assault deep into Lebanon, scattering the PLO; but up to 1979, and even beyond, there were grounds for United States optimism concerning a Middle-East settlement.[3]

In South-East Asia, too, the US position had shown some improvement since the fall of Saigon, and by 1978 talks were under way on American economic assistance to Vietnam. It was precisely at this moment that things began to go badly wrong for the United States. One of the great diplomatic problems of the era of *détente* for US administrations had been how to maintain progressively improving relations with two powers—Russia and China—which were antipathetic towards each other. Now in December 1978, as a second series of strategic arms limitation talks reached its climax, the United States at last normalized diplomatic relations with the People's Republic of China and almost simultaneously launched a programme of increased military expenditure at home. United States negotiations on aid to Vietnam were abruptly broken off, and in February 1979 China invaded her southern neighbour, intent on curbing Vietnamese traditional ambitions to dominate Kampuchea and the whole of former French Indo-China. Only the previous month the Middle East balance had been upset and US–Soviet relations threatened as the Shah of Iran, a long-standing ally of the United States, was forced into exile after months of revolutionary unrest.[4] Past Soviet and Cuban involvement in the Horn of Africa at one and the same time fed US fears of Soviet ambitions in Iran and the Gulf and ensured that American attempts to find alternative military bases in the area were almost bound to tread on Russian toes. The Rubicon had been crossed, and neither of the superpowers any longer felt that much was to be gained by thinking well of the other. SALT II foundered. The US announced its intention to site Pershing nuclear missiles in Europe and increase military spending. Its allies were urged to follow suit. Talk of the possibility of winning a nuclear war became more and more frequent in the USA, though not in Europe. The British general election of 1979 and the US presidential election of the following year showed a marked tilt to the right in public opinion and served to legitimize a revival of fully-fledged Cold War rhetoric. At the close of the year the Soviet Union had little hesitation in sending its troops into Afghanistan to protect a progressive but hopelessly ham-fisted regime from its own people.[5]

Departures and Divisions in the Third World

This cooling of great power relations had a considerable effect on the Third World and the North–South dialogue. It reduced the prominence of development problems without lessening their severity. It led DC governments to accompany their continuing unwillingness to compromise with a much more aggressively individualist and libertarian rhetoric than before, which was not infrequently enlisted in support of tougher policies. It prompted renewed and often quixotic thoughts of regional economic integration, southern autonomy, and northern intervention as alternatives to continued negotiation in multilateral forums. Finally it created new sources of dissension and aggravated old divisions within the Group of 77. Let us take these in turn.

The very phrase 'North–South' had, of course, been coined to drum in the message that relations between the DCs of the West and the non-Communist LDCs had replaced superpower rivalry as the central concern of the UN system and the world's diplomats. Opinion in the DCs, on the Left as much as the Right, reacted to the renewal of East–West tension by a return to old preoccupations. The revival of the European disarmament movement, dormant for more than a decade, provides the clearest illustration of this. But there was a further reason why the North–South dialogue could no longer claim the attention of western publics so confidently. The crisis in Iran pushed oil prices up sharply once again. This new rise was met by the DCs to an even greater extent than in the mid-1970s with policies of tight monetary control. Inflation had been identified by western governments as a socially disruptive phenomenon to be avoided even at the cost of unemployment levels not seen since the 1930s. At one and the same time these deflationary policies curbed demand for third-world exports and fuelled nationalist campaigns for trade restrictions aimed at the highly competitive and allegedly disruptive NICs. Talk of the benefits of free trade fell unconvincingly from the lips of third-world publicists. The ingenuous stress of the Brandt Commission on the mutual interest of North and South in various policies of reform evoked little response in major western capitals and deserved less.[6]

There, indulgence had given way to impatience, reluctant tolerance to outright testiness. Aside from detailed shifts in the attitudes of northern states on particular North–South questions which will be considered in their place, this was manifested in two ways. First, as in the 1950s and 1960s, the new cold war was to serve as 'a highly functional system by which the superpowers control their own domains'.[7] The Americans in El Salvador would legitimize their repressive policing by pointing to the threat of Soviet expansionism; the Soviets, with as little evidence, would justify military rule in Poland by talk of US imperialism and intrigue, when both countries were plainly in the grip of autochthonous movements which their powerful neighbours were set on stifling. Second, liberal ideologies were ready to fuel a moral counter-attack on the various justifications put forward by the Third World for a NIEO. The comforting analogy between rich and poor in the national community and rich and poor states in the world community had seemed to suggest that just as western bourgeoisies in an interdependent capitalist society had found it politic and right to concede to the demands of their poor for welfare states, so, now, equivalent claims had come into being against rich states because of the high and growing level of integration in the world economy. This was now dismissed as poor history and sloppy thinking. States might be juridical individuals but they were not moral individuals. The ultimate source of what sympathy there might be in the North for the plight of the South lay in the extreme poverty of individual men, women, and children, not the budgetary dilemmas of states; yet it was to be states that would benefit from the various measures comprising the NIEO, it has been the economic rights and duties of states, not individuals, which had been proclaimed by the UN General Assembly, and there was no guarantee whatsoever that democratic donors might not inadvertently diminish the welfare of individuals in the Third World by strengthening authoritarian regimes there.[8] This stress on individual human rights, though well meant, provided the United States and other western governments with a convenient stick with which to beat the USSR and selected third-world states, while turning a blind eye to the sins of their allies.

Another issue offering comparable ironies was nuclear proliferation. In 1968 a Treaty on the Non-Proliferation of Nuclear Weapons (NPT) negotiated under UN auspices had been opened for signature. In essence it was a bargain struck between the superpowers and the wealthier LDCs. The latter would accept international controls on civil nuclear programmes to prevent the spread of nuclear weapons; the former would offer assistance with the peaceful application of nuclear technology and take steps toward mutually agreed arms reduction. The NPT was not universally accepted. France expressed the intention of abiding by the treaty but would not sign it. The Chinese took an explicitly third-world line, objecting to the élitist character of a pact which limited the sovereignty of non- and near-nuclear weapons states disproportionately. Predictably, other major third-world states agreed, and in discussions within the UN up to and including the first review conference of the NPT, held in 1975, Mexico, Yugoslavia, and India were prominent critics of the failure of the superpowers to disarm and the inadequate scale of assistance in connection with peaceful use of nuclear power. Then, in May 1974, India injected a new urgency into the proliferation debate by exploding a nuclear device which had been developed by clandestine diversion of fissile material from its Canadian-supplied civil programme.[9]

By 1975, therefore, non-proliferation was already a North–South issue, but notwithstanding southern complaints, it was one on which the USA had shown considerable goodwill. US policy had consistently favoured the spread of peaceful nuclear technology, and had accepted that this would naturally lead to more and more countries possessing their own nuclear fuel reprocessing plants under International Atomic Energy Authority (IAEA) supervision, even though it was precisely this technology which would enable any state so minded to produce nuclear weapons. Then, as the perception of deteriorating security took hold of the official mind, the US position hardened. Higher oil prices had resulted in increased investment in nuclear power generation. By 1975 competition between rival exporters appeared to be resulting in concessions on safeguards as French and German firms offered to supply enrichment and reprocessing plants as well as reactors to South Korea, Iran, and Pakistan. Although deals of this kind fell within the terms of the NPT they proved too much for US nerves in the new and more tense atmosphere of the later 1970s. The Americans accordingly tried with some success to block the French and German deals and in 1975 organized a Nuclear Suppliers Group (NSG) which privately drafted new and more stringent rules to limit technology exports. On nuclear proliferation, as on human rights, President Carter attempted to project US policy in moral terms with much talk of the danger of nuclear weapons falling into irresponsible hands. His election was accordingly followed in 1977 by cutbacks in US nuclear technology exports and by vigorous use of the threat of suspension of supplies of enriched uranium as a means of securing compliance with more restrictive policies.[10] No more third-world states seriously threatened to embark on nuclear welfare in 1977 than had done ten years before when the NPT was concluded, yet the combination of patronizing declaration and abrasive bullying, of naïvety and calculation, which characterized US policy had served so to embitter relations with major third-world states on this issue by the latter date that the obvious functional question of the public good of non-proliferation had been quite lost sight of. Pleading global security, the USA had ridden roughshod over the sovereignty of those in whose interests it claimed to act. In doing so it threatened to undermine a treaty of which it was itself the chief beneficiary.

A further consequence of renewed East–West tension was to toss into the air once again the perennial question of economic regionalism. For many years there had been those who were willing to detect in any step along the road of European integration, however halting, an anti-American conspiracy or the birth of a new superpower. Thought on these lines had been encouraged by a temporary US loss of confidence in the mid-1970s and the enlargement of the EEC, by the acceleration of European DFI in the seventies after two decades in which US firms had seemed impregnable, and by the refusal of France to toe the American line after the OPEC action of 1973–4. At the heart of the EEC had been a compromise whereby Germany had agreed to accept French agricultural goods in exchange for agreement to a common market for manufactured goods which would favour German exports to France. This had left no place for traditional US exports of agricultural goods to Europe and laid the basis for an expansion of intra-EEC (the Six) exports from 30 per cent of total exports in 1958 to 49 per cent by 1970.[11]

In the relaxed conditions of the 1970s, US administrations could live with the notion of high degrees of European and Japanese autonomy. But towards the end of the decade it was felt to be vital to United States interests to reaffirm control over these allies, to secure their co-operation in the siting of strategic weapons and their commitment to increased military expenditure. This difficult process of regaining lapsed authority had direct consequences for the international economic order.

Trade negotiations came to be used as bones of contention, suitably remote from the leading issues of military policy, over which commitment and loyalty could be tested out. Growing protectionist sentiment at all levels both in Europe and the USA made it easy for officials to build up elaborate wrangles over US petrochemicals-based exports, European steel exports, and agricultural policy: issues which, while intrinsically important, served the ulterior purpose of signalling across the Atlantic the mood of the major NATO allies and the sorts of reactions to be expected on yet more contentious matters such as the US attempt to place an embargo on European sales of equipment for the new Soviet gas pipeline as punishment for the alleged Soviet role in the Polish clampdown of 1981.

This more aggressive phase in trade negotiations between the leading western economies might be expected to constrain their freedom to negotiate with the South. Alternatively, it might prompt leading economies to reaffirm control over their spheres of influence —the US in Latin America, Europe in Africa—in ways which might provide leverage for favoured third-world states but would be just as likely to narrow third-world freedom of action. Finally, and in conjunction with a heightening of regional tensions, the new phase of northern protectionism might be expected to prompt fresh thought about the viability of third-world integration as a route away from northern intransigence and northern battles.

The gestures of ASEAN in this direction seem insubstantial as yet. In the Middle East and South Asia, the fall of the Shah of Iran removed a most vociferous advocate of economic integration and brought down a number of interesting ventures.[12] At the same time, however, it went some way to depoliticize integration, which had rightly been suspected as a vehicle for Iranian imperialism. In Latin America, where integration on an inappropriately European model had been pioneered in the 1950s, the impotence of ANCOM after the Chilean defection of 1976 and the disbanding of LAFTA in 1980 might seem to have signalled an end to thoughts of integration. Yet one of the most pregnant innovations of the new Latin American Integration Association (LAIA) which has replaced LAFTA is its abandonment of the most-favoured-nation principle, which had prevented sub-groups within the old Association from negotiating exclusive mutual concessions. Argentina, the principal architect of the shift in integration policy, looks forward to 'closer economic cooperation among countries with homogeneous structures and economic policies' within LAIA, founded on 'an ample base of shared values and interests'.[13] Diana Tussie, in a recent examination of the significance of the switch from LAFTA to LAIA, adds that 'the swing to the right of the Southern Republics coupled with the increasing influence of orthodox [liberal] economic policy-makers seem to provide precisely the "base of shared values and interests" that such a project of an economic community requires'.[14] This suggests an attempt to use the substantially increased if volatile exchange reserves built up by some of the major Latin American states by resort to the Euromarkets during the 1970s to break away from the old *dirigiste* notion of integration as import substitution writ large, in favour of a more right-wing variant which placed much greater emphasis on the value of internal competition and the need for improved access to DC markets.

Even more inchoate than the various regional moves are the wider global initiatives in the direction of improved inter-regional southern co-operation or South–South relations, which welled up as frustration with North–South discussions grew after 1977.[15] Two UN initiatives explored one important aspect of this theme. The first, the UN Conference on Technical Co-operation among Developing Countries (UNCTCDC) took place in Buenos Aires in September 1978. In a replay of UNCTAD I the Group of 77 sought and secured the institutionalization of this conference, much against the wishes of the DCs, so creating a permanent UN body with access to UN Development Programme funds devoted to the exchange of technology between third-world countries, the substitution of home-grown technology for allegedly inappropriately capital-intensive technologies exported by the DCs, and the creation of autonomous research facilities in the Third World.[16] Two months later at an international forum on appropriate technology organized by the UN Industrial Development Organization (UNIDO) in New Delhi, a similar stress on indigenous third-world values and skills and a more cautious attitude to imported technology was again apparent.[17]

It remained to be determined how far this new movement would develop into a recrudescence of Indian Swadeshi thinking, with its stress on small-scale ingenious peasant solutions to modern problems, and how far it might serve instead as a convenient mask for the spread of new, profit-oriented and NIC-based MNCs into less-rapidly developing LDCs, to provide production-lines, urban utilities, and consumer products only marginally better attuned to third-world markets than those of the DCs.[18]

The same frustration at the failure of the CIEC and the seizing up of the wider North–South dialogue, which prompted renewed discussion of regional integration and the vogue for southern technical co-operation, also led to demands for more effective southern negotiating capability and the creation of a southern secretariat independent of UNCTAD.[19] While part of the impetus for this demand came from past failures, and part from the very real difficulties facing the smaller LDCs, with few technically expert negotiators, in their attempts to participate in the many-faceted dialogue, an ulterior motive was the need to distract attention from the growing evidence of dissension within the Group of 77 while at the same time creating a body which might help in future to disguise differences of interest by more careful preparatory work before major conferences.

These growing disagreements, like so many aspects of the politics of the later 1970s, were inextricably bound up with the decay in US–Soviet and Sino–Soviet relations and the multiple crises to which this decay gave rise in Iran, in Arab–Egyptian relations, and in South-East Asia.

The Group of 77 had never been free from dissension. Beneath the rather sterile facade of the block vote in the UN it was possible to distinguish three sub-groups within the Group—the Latin Americans, the Muslim community, and a group of poorer, mostly African and Caribbean LDCs. Perhaps more significant than this was the fact that some of the most wealthy and powerful LDCs turned out to be divided in their loyalties. Powers, in his study of the 1975 General Assembly, found that Argentina, Brazil, Singapore, and India all failed to align clearly with any of the three LDC groupings.[20]

Clear public expression of these potential cleavages was by and large restrained during the mid-1970s but exploded in 1979. Ironically this happened first in the Non-Aligned Movement (NAM) which had originated in the efforts of Nasser, Nehru, Tito, Sukarno, and Bandaranaike to retain independence of action at the height of the Cold War and was dedicated to the autonomy of the Third World from struggles between the great powers. Under Algerian chairmanship between 1973 and 1976, the NAM had performed an important role in formulating third-world positions on NIEO as much as on security questions, but during 1979 its effectiveness was threatened precisely by the great-power alignments of key members. Many member states objected to the forthcoming assumption of the chair by Cuba, which was widely felt to be unacceptably close to the Soviet Union, and in May 1979 rumours circulated of African plans to prevent Cuba from hosting the September summit meeting of the Movement, while the Indian government expressed fears of a split.[21] Cuba, for its part, condemned other members for their close links with the USA, and the Arab states, following the treaty with Israel, seemed intent on ousting Egypt. Inevitably there was disagreement over which of the two rival Kampuchean regimes should be accepted. As if this were not enough, African and Latin American tempers were frayed following further uncompensated OPEC price rises resulting from the Iranian crisis and a mild recovery in the OECD states. In spite of attempts at conciliation beforehand, notably by the ageing pioneer of non-alignment, Tito, the Havana summit was an uneasy event.[22] Cuban stage-management was evident and main issues—Kampuchea and Egypt—were left for consideration by the Foreign Ministers' meeting scheduled for New Delhi in 1981 in the reasonable hope that by then the passage of time might have removed the source of disagreement.[23] Although many sympathized with a suggestion by the Burmese foreign minister that the best thing might be to disband and start again, his was the only state to leave the movement.[24]

Discontent within the NAM was directly attributable to the decay of great-power relations. Discontent within the Group of 77 over higher oil prices owed more to the domestic crisis in Iran, though this had been aggravated considerably by US policy. Its wider political significance lay less in its origins than in the manner in which it threatened to undermine the Arab position on the Palestinian question.

Discontent was made public at UNCTAD V in Manila when Alfonso Rudas of Colombia attacked OPEC and demanded that petroleum be brought within UNCTAD's mandate.[25] Two months later, in July 1979, the Organization of African Unity (OAU) expressed its discontent with the lack of effective compensation received by a majority of its members for oil price rises by refusing to condemn Egyptian policy towards Israel and instead giving President Sadat a standing ovation.[26] In August Zaïre applied further pressure by announcing that it was considering a resumption of diplomatic relations with Israel.[27] By the end of 1979 there were no more than tentative indications of Arab response to this deterioration in political grip, though non-Arab members of OPEC, including Nigeria and Venezuela had taken some positive steps.[28]

And all of these aggravations of political cleavages in the Third World came at the end of a decade which had seen the economic development paths of a dozen or so NICs diverge markedly from those of the greater number of poorer, primary-commodity exporting LDCs, reducing rather than increasing the rather tenuous community of economic interest which had first bound the Group of 77 together in pursuit of reform some fifteen years before.

The Committee of the Whole and the Brandt Commission

In spite of all these difficulties, attempts to sustain southern initiatives of 1973 and 1974 continued to the end of the decade and beyond. There was, though, some shift in stress away from grandiose all-embracing negotiations to narrower functional arenas. This arose partly from the failure of the CIEC, which found no immediate successor, partly from the growing importance of the continuing committee and conference work of UNCTAD relative to its quadrennial full sessions, and partly from the coincidental occurrence of a number of functionally limited but vastly complicated negotiations, including the final stages of UNCLOS III and the Tokyo Round, during the closing years of the decade.

Yet the grand tradition epitomized by the CIEC was sustained, albeit with reduced expectations, in two contrasting forums. Disillusioned by the failure of a smaller group of states to make any significant new compromises in the CIEC, the Group of 77 used its vote in the General Assembly of the United Nations to throw out a proposal from the DCs that the North–South dialogue be continued in some similarly select body and resolved instead to establish a Committee of the Whole, open to all members of the General Assembly, for this purpose. This was in 1977. Two years later the General Assembly reaffirmed the preference of its dominant LDC majority for universal negotiation by designating the Committee of the Whole as preparatory committee for a planned round of Global Negotiations on international economic co-operation.[29] A contrasting response to the 1977 stalemate in overall discussions on the NIEO was the suggestion from Robert McNamara that former Chancellor Willy Brandt of West Germany should head an Independent Commission on International Development, soon to become known as the Brandt Commission, to generate proposals on the reduction of North–South confrontation. Excluding only the centrally-planned economies, Brandt strove to bring together elder statesmen and men and women of stature from Chile, Britain, Tanzania, Kuwait, Colombia, Upper Volta, the USA (two members), India, Indonesia, France, Canada, Sweden, Guyana, Japan, and Algeria. Starting work at Schloss Gymnich, near Bonn, in December 1977, they were to report directly to the UN Secretary General in 1980.

The result was a report which was as careless in its assumptions as it was unrealistic in its proposals. That poverty leads to war, that states have rights, let alone equal rights, that 'all cultures deserve equal respect, protection and promotion', that imperatives 'rooted in the hard-headed self-interest of all countries . . . reinforce the claim of human solidarity', and that rationality is a precondition of survival are all intriguing and plausible propositions for each of which there is much to be said, but every one of them is open to such cogent objections that its emphatic and unqualified insertion among the premises of the Brandt Report could serve only to sow doubt in the mind of the reader. It might just as easily have been argued that it is changes in the economic welfare of nations rather than absolute poverty which incline them to war, that the problematic notion of individual rights cannot survive translation into states' rights, that cultural relativism is no more than a symptom of moral bankruptcy, that the interests of states are sometimes irreconcilable, and that rationality, however commendable, places one at a disadvantage.[30]

The presumptive method of the Commission was most clearly evident in its adherence to the notion of mutuality of interest between North and South from the very start, before any discussions had taken place. Yet once the idealistic premise of ultimate harmony of interests is accepted, it follows that reform becomes a process less of creation than of rediscovery and restoration, in which the grime of centuries is gradually dissolved until the original well-composed picture is revealed. 'Ought' and 'must' slip unobserved into the discourse of the reformer and multiply there, seeming sufficient in themselves to remove political obstacles which are, by definition, the aberrant and misinformed acts of wayward states as yet not fully aware of their best interests. Like all such tracts, the Report allows its own low evaluation of the barriers in the way of international development to preclude serious discussion of means. Indeed the initial identification of ends and the creation of political will to achieve them come to be conceived of as the only important means, and all the rest—the peculiarity of institutions, the complexity of issues, the logic of negotiation, the imperfection of communications, the mutual inconsistency of objectives, the private ambitions of public figures, and a host of domestic constraints on foreign policy —are either ignored or else dismissed as technicalities and details. In political reform, tactics and mundane details are as essential as long-term objectives, yet the report shows no awareness of this, no real concern for feasibility or procedure, and has for this reason quickly faded into obscurity in spite of the commendability of many of its specific recommendations.[31]

The Common Fund

The creation of the Committee of the Whole and the deliberations of the Brandt Commission represented respectively the preferred southern and northern methods of achieving a decisive breakthrough in North–South relations, but the gains of this period, slight as they were, are to be looked for elsewhere. At Nairobi, UNCTAD had received a mandate to hold major negotiations on the Common Fund, debt relief, and the transfer of technology. The agreement to establish a Common Fund under the IPC had indeed appeared the single most important outcome of UNCTAD IV in 1976, yet four years were to pass before a substantial agreement was initialled giving shape to the originally ill-defined concept.

A first negotiating conference, held during March and April 1977, was regarded by the Brazilian representative as a 'complete failure', and agreed only to meet again in November.[32] The second session of the negotiating conference fared little better, and talks broke down completely, only to be resumed a year later after a good deal of to-ing and fro-ing by UNCTAD Secretary-General Gamani Corea and some signs of British support in Commonwealth discussions had suggested that the climate of opinion might have changed just enough to bring forth an acceptable compromise.[33]

Disagreement centred upon four main issues. How was the fund to be financed? How was it to relate to ICAs? What if anything was to be provided to assist commodities which could not be stockpiled through the so-called Second Window of the Fund? How was the Fund to be governed?

The Group of 77 and the UNCTAD secretariat had thought from the start of a fund in the region of $6 billion of which one-third would consist of direct government contributions while the remainder would be raised by the issue of bonds. The DCs, by contrast, envisaged a much more modest fund with which individual ICA managers would deposit 75 per cent of their funds, receiving in return a right to draw when additional funds were needed to stabilize the market for their particular commodity. Aside from a very small amount of money for initial office expenses there would be no direct government contributions, nor were the DCs sympathetic to a Second Window to provide concessional development assistance to exporters of non-storable commodities. In their view, all elements of aid must be excluded if a Common Fund were to be able to perform its central stabilizing role effectively. A Fund which channelled money into development projects or tried to sustain commodity prices at levels above the long-term trend would prove unable to borrow in commercial markets and would harm the interests of net importers of primary commodities.

With UNCTAD V only six months away, the Group of 77 and the UNCTAD secretariat were keen to try to negotiate their way to something which could be held up as a solid achievement on the road to a NIEO when the Common Fund talks resumed in November 1978. Yet little more came out of this meeting than a more precisely quantified statement of the gulf which still separated the USA and Germany from the Group of 77. It is true that by now the DCs had accepted the notion of some direct government contributions to the Fund, perhaps as much as $230,000 per state, but this was little more than half the level contemplated by the LDCs. It is true that the DCs had conceded that there should be a Second Window, but the gesture was an empty one since they insisted that contributions to it should be voluntary.[34] It is true, finally, that the USA was now prepared to accept that as little as 40 per cent of the maximum financial requirement of each ICA be deposited in cash with the Fund, but this was still too high for the Group of 77.[35] So once again talks ended in a thinly disguised failure, leaving all to be resolved at a final session in March 1979.

Nothing indicates more clearly than the timing of the final agreement on the Common Fund in March 1979 the opportunist and conspiratorial nature of North–South relations. The South wanted a success that could be flourished at the Manila UNCTAD in May as evidence that the North–South dialogue was still progressing. The North did not want the bother of a public failure. Both sides therefore found a formula which looked like a compromise between negotiating positions and was presented as such, although it was a virtual defeat for the South.

The terms of the Geneva package were hardly generous. The First Window of the Fund was to amount to $150 million in cash contributions from governments, with a further $300 million on call or in the form of government guarantees against which funds might be raised in the market. Payments of $70 million to the Second Window were promised, and a more ambitious notional target set of $300 million. The LDCs were obliged to concede that responsibility for the management of price stability should rest with the individual ICAs, with the Common Fund playing a passive, supportive role. Each ICA in the IPC was to deposit one-third of its maximum financial requirement with the Fund. Finally, voting power driving from direct contributions was to be disproportionate to contributions, with the Group of 77 controlling 47 per cent and Group B only 42 per cent of these votes.

These last two items of agreement represented concessions to the Group of 77 position. A third of the maximum financial requirement of each ICA was very much less than the USA had wished to see deposited, and the break with the Bretton Woods principle of voting in strict proportion to financial contributions was reported as a great victory for the South. 'Several Third World delegates were openly jubilant about the voting formula', wrote Ian Guest, 'which they feel could well spell an end to the West's domination in international institutions'.[36]

More sober reflection soon showed that little of substance had been conceded. Decisions on expenditure required a three-quarters majority and other decisions a two-thirds majority, so that a coalition of leading DCs would still retain an effective veto. More than this, the whole agreement was tentative. It could be wheeled out as a symbol of the coming NIEO at Manila, as indeed it was, but it still depended, like any international treaty or convention, on a lengthy process of ratification by national governments and legislatures before it could come into force, and even then it would depend for its effectiveness on the number of ICAs affiliating to it, the goodwill of states in making voluntary contributions to the Second Window, the judgement of world capital markets on its bonds, and the solidarity of the Group of 77 in the face of an apparent success which many of its members were coming to believe would do them more harm than good.

Individual Commodity Negotiations

Concerning ratification, DC voluntary contributions, and the solidarity of the Group of 77, only time would tell, but by the time the Common Fund agreement was finally initialled in Geneva in June 1979 there were already strong indications that the strenuous programme of negotiations on individual commodities hosted by UNCTAD over the past three years was in disarray.

Discussions on copper had begun in November 1976, but the presence of large numbers of marginal participants and the lack of enthusiasm of the two major exporters, Chile and Zaïre, for the UNCTAD forum combined with the technical characteristics of copper made a favourable outcome improbable.[37] Copper meetings during 1977 and 1978 drifted steadily towards the creation of a consultative intergovernmental body which might even be autonomous from UNCTAD.[38]

In 1977 a new International Sugar Agreement to come into force at the beginning of 1978 was concluded under UNCTAD auspices, but it centred upon a system of export quotas and nationally held and financed stocks which was entirely inconsistent with the Common Fund idea.[39] Nor was it very satisfactory even as an independent agreement. The EEC, which had expanded production following the high sugar prices of 1973–4, would not accept that its re-exports of cane sugar from the ACP countries under Protocol 3 of the Lomé Convention should be included in its ISA export quota. No compromise was found, and the EEC therefore remained outside the agreement, expanding its subsidized exports of high-cost domestically produced beet sugar during the sustained period of low free-market prices in the late 1970s, even when the signatories of the ISA had cut back their own agreed export quotas by almost 20 per cent in a vain effort to hold prices. Moreover because the stock financing fund envisaged in the new ISA was not due to come into operation until the agreement had been ratified, and because US ratification in the shape of a Sugar Bill was stuck fast in the gullet of Congress throughout 1978 and up to its eventual defeat in October 1979, the International Sugar Organization was obliged to meet the crisis with one arm tied behind its back. Not until late 1979 did sugar prices rise above the ISA floor of 11 US cents per lb. and the prospects for US ratification brighten.[40]

US tardiness in ratifying the ISA cannot be put down to intransigence on North–South issues. Dispute in Congress centred upon the support price to be paid to US farmers for their output of beet sugar and was plainly an embarrassment to the Carter administration, which had declared itself to be in favour of ICAs for selected commodities, including sugar. But the USA was a wittingly disruptive force in several other sets of negotiations on UNCTAD core commodities at this time.

The adherence of the United States for the first time to the fifth International Tin Agreement was a mixed blessing. In June 1978 the *Financial Times* reported Malaysian discontent with US behaviour. Deputy Minister for Primary Industries, Paul Leong, was said to have claimed that 'since the entry of new consuming members, particularly the US . . . consumers tended to flex their muscles and pursue a confrontation course with producers'.[41] The Malaysian attack continued the following month when Rahim Aki, President of the Chamber of Mines, complained that the principle of decision by consensus on which the first four ITAs had operated had now given way to constant voting because of the new, aggressive attitude of consumers.[42] Behind these public attacks lay continuing concern at the ability of the United States, through its strategic stockpile, to manipulate the market at a time when the ITO, after a long period during which prices had been above the ITA ceiling, had no effective means of controlling the market. Towards the end of 1979, as a US bill to authorize stockpile sales creaked its way through Congress, knocking tin prices this way and that as its prospects of success first rose, then fell, then rose again, the irritation of the exporting countries was very understandable and seemed bound to sour negotiations for the sixth ITA, due to start in 1980. From the point of view of UNCTAD, these events were doubly depressing: first because any breakdown in this most long-lived of ICAs would be a serious psychological defeat for the IPC, and second because the whole ITA process remained resolutely independent from the UNCTAD IPC. Producers were opposed to any link with the Common Fund, which they feared might make it more difficult for the ITA to raise and use money because of the complex and restrictive decision-making procedures of the Fund.[43]

Coffee prices, after reaching an all-time peak in the second quarter of 1977, had fallen into a steady decline thereafter, placing great strain on the recently concluded International Coffee Agreement. Repeated demands in the International Coffee Organization from exporters for a higher trigger price to bring into action ICA quota reductions were met by consumer intransigence, led by the USA.[44] Consumers argued that falling prices were not the same as low prices and that the market should be allowed to readjust after the quite abnormal shortages which had followed the Brazilian frosts of July 1975. There was no reason to revise the ICA price band agreed prior to the frosts. Producers responded with non-ICA measures to keep coffee off the market. An export ban introduced by Central American states in March 1978, undermined by Guatemalan and Salvadorean free-riding, was lifted the following month. Brazil attempted to influence the market through a closely administered system of export prices and taxes, but an acceleration in the price-fall in the third quarter of the year brought rumours of collective action by producers in August 1978.[45] These were confirmed in November, when Latin American producers meeting in Guatemala City agreed to set up a $140 million fund to support coffee prices. As 1979 progressed it became clear that concerted action by producers, united in what had become known as the Bogota Group, was no mere flash in the pan. Their intervention was widely believed to have kept prices as much as 30 cents per lb. higher than they would otherwise have been, and this caused very considerable ill-feeling in the USA.[46] There was also talk of Indonesia and the Ivory Coast joining the group.[47] Yet this drift toward collective consumer action was of little comfort to the UNCTAD secretariat, since it offered no prospect of a buffer stock fund under the ICA which might affiliate to the Common Fund. Moreover, coffee producers had publicly expressed their disdain for the IPC. In July 1979 Julio Turbay Ayala, President of one of the leading coffee exporting states, Colombia, declared that 'for me, the appropriate forum for the discussion of each primary product is the corresponding individual agreement'. He continued, 'I believe the consolidation of each agreement . . . represents the best policy for cooperation between developed and developing countries'.[48]

Cocoa appeared for some time to be one of the IPC's strongest prospects. The first international agreement had been reached in 1972. A second pact, to run for three years from the end of September 1976, had been agreed in 1975, and was being renegotiated under UNCTAD auspices with United States participation. In addition, the low level of the price range in the 1975 Agreement had meant that funds accumulating from export levies raised by producer states to finance buffer stock purchases to defend the floor price of 55 (later 75) cents per kilo had never been used. At $200 million the cocoa fund could prove a substantial depositor with the Common Fund.[49] Yet as with tin, US participation was no unmixed blessing, for although the adherence of a state which was far and away the leading importer ought to strengthen any new agreement, it was apparent that the US delegation was making negotiations more difficult by widening the range of disagreement on a number of issues.[50] When UNCTAD talks on the new cocoa pact broke down in December because of a total failure to reach a compromise on the price range to be defended, it appeared that US participation had backfired badly and that yet another primary commodity was slipping out of the IPC. If no fresh agreement were concluded, the $200 million fund would be returned to the producer states, and it seemed probable, following their December meeting in Abidjan, that they would use the money in imitation of the currently successful Bogota Group to support prices and manage the market quite independently both of the importing states and the UNCTAD secretariat.

Indeed by the end of 1979 the only one of the ten IPC core commodities which remained within the UNCTAD fold and reasonably firmly on course was rubber. This had been the first commodity to reach the stage of a formal negotiating conference within the IPC framework in September 1978. As in so many other sets of negotiations in this period, it was the USA which adopted the role of hard man on behalf of the consumer states in opposition to a closely-knit group of LDC exporters, mostly in South-East Asia, which had formed themselves into the Association of Natural Rubber Producing Countries (ANRPC) in November 1976. US negotiators characteristically argued for a larger buffer stock and a lower floor price than the producers wanted, and opposed any suggestion of export quotas or taxes to influence the market.[51] The American position was that export controls could be used to rig the market in the short term and thus trigger upward revision of the price range which the buffer-stock manager was to defend.[52]

In spite of these disagreements the main lines of a rubber pact were agreed by April 1979, promising a deposit with the Common Fund in the region of $140 million.[53] Last minute US demands produced further delay, but the International Natural Rubber Agreement (INRA) was finally initialled in October 1979. Yet even this isolated IPC success was conditional upon the customary ratification procedures. It would come into force provisionally at the beginning of October 1980 if states responsible for 65 per cent of world exports and imports had ratified. It would not come fully into force, nor would the buffer-stock fund come into operation, until states responsible for 80 per cent of world exports and imports had ratified, and a further six months, to the beginning of April 1981, were allowed for this.

By 1980, therefore, prospects of further progress in the IPC were slight. Talks on three of the ten core commodities—tea, cotton, and coffee were openly unsympathetic to UNCTAD objectives, and the coffee producers, along with cocoa exporting countries, were moving in the direction of producer cartel arrangements that would make future links with a Common Fund still less probable. Finally, an interminable US ratification procedure had considerably weakened the International Sugar Agreement and ought to have muted any jubilation felt by UNCTAD staff over the as yet un-ratified rubber agreement of 1979. Many of the eight non-core IPC commodities were still poorly organized, though a new olive oil agreement to continue the 1963 agreement had been opened for signature in April 1979 and included a symbolic commitment to the Common Fund.

UNCTAD: Debt Relief, Transfer of Technology, UNCTAD V

UNCTAD was not solely concerned with primary commodities. Debt relief had been studied by officials since the early 1970s and rose to prominence in 1976. At Nairobi the Group of 77 pressed for debt relief for all countries facing difficulties in repayment and service, total cancellation of the debts of certain least-developed, landlocked, and island economies, and consolidation and rescheduling over a minimum of twenty-five years of the growing volume of LDC debts to private banks. The DCs were at first unsympathetic, but softened later, perhaps feeling that a tactical concession on debt, where the ultimate power to refuse repayment lay with the debtor, could be used to deflect pressure away from institutions such as the IMF, about which they were less keen to negotiate.[54] Negotiations in the CIEC and the UNCTAD Trade and Development Board led to a compromise in March 1978. Aid donors agreed to bring outstanding official obligations of the poorest states into line with the softer terms currently being given on new loans. The Group of 77 accepted the northern preference for *ad hoc* treatment of the debt problem by allowing reference to generalized debt relief to be suppressed.[55] Lenders agreed only to 'seek to adopt measures' so that it was some months before precise policy changes were announced, and these varied from one DC to another. The Dutch, Canadians, Swedes, and Swiss had already acted in advance of the negotiations. Many major powers were more cautious, however, feeling the effect of wholesale cancellations on the sanctity of contract. In July 1978 the British government announced that it was writing off £928 million owed by countries with low per capita incomes, almost three-quarters of it accounted for by India and Pakistan, and that future official assistance to these states would be in grant form. True to the new temper of the time, serious alleged violators of human rights, including Uganda and South Yemen, were excluded. Towards the end of the year a number of other major donors including West Germany, Japan, and the USA announced similar proposals, but all of this left untouched the mounting debt problems of the wealthier NICs, while the USA continued to resist UNCTAD demands for a new debt commission which would erode the authority of the IMF.[56]

Another issue on which UNCTAD IV had secured a firm mandate was the code of conduct on the transfer of technology. But although an intergovernmental group of experts charged with the negotiation of this code met seven times between November 1976 and November 1978, it failed to agree on key points, so that here, as in the Common Fund talks, all remained to be settled as UNCTAD V approached.[57] The Group of 77 complained that LDCs were necessarily at a disadvantage when negotiating the purchase of technology from DC firms because the knowledge embodied in the machinery and other artefacts that they were seeking to acquire was itself essential to the making of a rational decision on its value.[58] Together with the frequently monopolistic power of the sellers, this essentially logical difficulty had resulted in a condition of technological dependence. The Third World paid too much for technology in the form of royalties and licensing fees, and the technology it bought sometimes turned out to be inappropriate. Moreover, MNCs operating in the Third World often preferred to import new technology and products from their parent firms rather than carry out research and production locally, so that there seemed no prospect of LDCs gradually developing an autonomous technological community capable of generating processes and products tailored to local needs. UNCTAD officials set the cost of technological dependence at over $30 billion a year and contrasted this with a mere $2 billion spent by LDCs on independent research each year.[59]

The position by UNCTAD V in May 1979 may be summed up as follows. A number of initiatives of the early and mid-1970s had now reached an advanced stage of negotiation or simply awaited ratification. The Common Fund and the Liner Code fell into the second category, the codes on the transfer of technology and restrictive business practices into the former. Yet other NIEO negotiations appeared to be proceeding in a slow but orderly fashion toward settlement in the World Intellectual Property Organization (WIPO) and UNCLOS, under the watchful eye of the UNCTAD secretariat. There was little that could be done to expedite any of these negotiations in a full session of UNCTAD, and the purpose of such sessions had indeed become less clear. This was reflected in the proceedings, as the Group of 77 devoted much of its attention to unsuccessful attempts to initiate high-level discussion of fundamental structural reform of the world economy, to secure the creation of an international debt commission to oversee the mounting debt service problems of the Third World, and to win for UNCTAD an enlarged mandate to police protectionist measures adopted by the DCs.

The North was in no mood to permit the proliferation of overlapping institutions and firmly resisted these proposals; but on the last issue, that of protection, a seemingly modest final resolution passed by consensus, which called on the Trade and Development Board to review new restrictions on LDC exports as in the past, was regarded by two commentators as one of the main achievements of UNCTAD V, because it committed the developed countries 'to the avoidance of protectionist measures against the products of developing countries and to the need for adjustment'.[60] Within the narrow institutional context of UNCTAD V this must seem an extravagant claim. The key to the significance of the resolution, and of the UNCTAD discussion on trade in manufactured goods, is to be looked for in the broader context of the North–South dialogue. As so often in the history of the debate, interplay of different forums and vagaries of timing had taken control; UNCTAD V had become, at the highest level of analysis, an episode in the closing stages of the Tokyo Round of the GATT.

The Conclusion of the Tokyo Round

Why should the GATT MTN have become a major issue in North–South relations? Part of the answer lies not in OPEC pressure but in the Tokyo Declaration of 1973 which had set out the objectives and ground rules of the negotiations. As well as searching for further cuts in tariffs, this seventh round of MTN was to attack the growing web of non-tariff barriers (NTB) which was threatening world trade. Moreover the Declaration made specific reference to the need to secure benefits for the LDCs, and, to facilitate this, opened up participation in the talks to all states, and not merely those which belonged to the GATT. This meant that, in theory at least, the many LDCs which had stayed outside would be able to put their case on the structural inequity of the world trade regime to DCs which had formally declared their opposition to the deleterious effects of protectionism on economic development.

This said, the talks were almost bound to remain dominated by the state of bilateral negotiations between the major trading nations: the USA, Japan, and the EEC (which negotiates as one state in the MTN). It was offers and counter-offers of these countries, and most of all of the USA, which dictated the pace of the Tokyo Round, leaving the LDCs the unenviable task of attempting at the very end of the negotiations to win modifications in a delicately balanced and hence inflexible compromise package already agreed between the major states. For this reason the predicament of the third-world states in the Tokyo Round is not easily understood without some familiarity with the fundamental debate between the USA and the EEC, which determined both the subject and the timing of the LDC challenge in 1978.

The USA had entered into the Tokyo Round determined to call the EEC to order after several years during which growing European abuse of GATT rules had been reluctantly tolerated. The illiberal Common Agricultural Policy (CAP) was one target. Another was the way in which the EEC had interpreted article XXIV of the GATT, permitting preferential trade agreements between states engaged in the creation of a customs union or free trade area, in such a way as to cover arrangements with Associates, such as Turkey, whose ultimate full EEC membership was unlikely. In addition, the USA took exception to the backdoor re-introduction of quantitative restrictions, forbidden under the GATT, through voluntary export restraint agreements or orderly marketing arrangements, whereby Japan and other fast-growing exporters were bullied into an informal quota system under threat of EEC sanctions which, if employed, would certainly have breached GATT rules. Finally, the USA objected to the growing use by governments in Europe and elsewhere of domestic subsidies which, though not specifically restricted to exports, had a significant effect on export prices. An example given by Victoria Curzon Price is the Michelin tyre plant established in Nova Scotia early in the 1970s. Here the Canadian government had provided very large subsidies, partly to create employment, but partly because Michelin planned to export 80 per cent of output to the USA, making a useful net contribution to the Canadian balance of payments. In such cases the US government took the view that it was entitled to impose countervailing duties (CVDs) to the extent of any subsidies. Others, including the EEC, alleged that the importing states must first establish that its domestic producers had suffered material injury from the subsidized imports, and must even then restrict CVDs to the amount of any subsidies received by the offending exporter which would not ordinarily be available to firms producing for the domestic market.[61]

It was the row over subsidies and countervailing duties which more than anything else determined the timing of the final negotiations of the Tokyo Round, because the US Trade Act by which Congress had authorized the Executive to participate in the MTN stipulated that CVDs must be imposed with full severity from the start of 1979 unless some agreement modifying the hardline US position had been reached in the meantime. Should this imposition of CVDs take place it would make agreement very much more difficult by galvanizing industry lobbies on both sides of the Atlantic. This threat hanging over what was generally felt to be the most important element in the set of codes and tariff agreements negotiated in the MTN forced a compromise early in 1979 after the disruption of the change of administration had finally been got out of the way. However the inability of the new government to cajole Congress into conceding a lower textile tariff and a waiver on the imposition of CVDs helped to ensure that the EEC got the better of its trading partner. Not only did the EEC establish that injury must be demonstrated before CVDs are imposed; it also frustrated US demands for improved international surveillance of national subsidy policies.[62] Most important of all, from the point of view of the LDCs, the United States was too heavily engaged on this issue to sustain fully its initial opposition to the demands of the EEC for legitimization of selectively applied and unilaterally declared safeguards against rapidly growing exporters.

As this victory for the *dirigiste* EEC over US liberalism took shape in 1978 the LDCs began to display agitation over its implications. For the US defeat was also a defeat for the more industrialized LDCs. What the USA had sought to defend on broad ideological grounds, the NICs stood to lose by very immediately, as it was against them, most of all, that the EEC intended to discriminate when applying safeguards. More in desperation than with any real hope of acceptance, the NICs suggested that the EEC might bind itself, when imposing selective curbs on imports, to apply them automatically not only to the target country but also to any other non-member states with an equal or greater share of the EEC market for the goods in question (usually the USA!).[63]

Though much weaker than the USA would have wished, the code on subsidies and CVDs also held dangers for the NICs, which perceived that many of their domestic policies might be found in breach of the rules in future, and argued ingeniously that they should be subject to less restrictive conditions than the DCs, since the subsidies they granted helped firms to battle against disadvantages while those granted by DC governments simply defended the dominance of established firms.[64]

LDC concern over the lack of strong measures to push along DC adjustment to the rapidly changing pattern of comparative advantage, over the too liberal treatment of MNCs in the code on customs valuation procedures, and over the details of the government procurement code, when added to much stronger dissatisfaction on anti-subsidy regulations and safeguards and a general resentment at being called upon in the closing weeks of negotiations to comment on a *fait accompli*, all added up to a third-world revolt which took place in April 1979, when the LDCs refused to sign the completed GATT package.

The purposes of this boycott were three. First of all, the Group of 77 wished to delay signature until after UNCTAD V in May so that they could use this favoured forum to voice their grievances on trade and win concessions, perhaps on quite different issues. Second, they hoped either within GATT itself or at UNCTAD V, to win specific concessions on trade—most of all a requirement that DCs should submit to clearance by a surveillance body before applying selective safeguards—as the price for their signatures. Third, there was not a great deal to be gained by kowtowing to an unsatisfactory compromise if it was never in fact going to take effect. It therefore seemed prudent to hang fire until the end of 1979, by which time they would have clearer indications of the attitude of US Congress known to be growing more protectionist by the hour.[65]

UNCTAD V passed without any substantial concessions, the US Congress began its deliberations, and the US and the EEC slipped further down the road towards trade war as charge and countercharge concerning the alleged dumping of US petroleum-derived goods and EEC steel and CAP goods passed across the Atlantic. Yet still, by mid-1980, even after months of deliberation in the special committee created in November 1979 to resolve it, the deadlock on safeguards continued with no final agreement on the criteria of market disruption or on arbitration procedures.[66] In the circumstances many LDCs were coming round to the view that the existing unreformed Article XIX of the GATT was perhaps to be preferred to any feasible replacement, and the major element of the GATT package accordingly remained unsettled more than a year after the talks proper had been brought to a close.

This disappointingly prolonged wrangle confirmed third-world perceptions of a deteriorating trading environment. In spite of a constant barrage of liberal argument from the secretariats of the OECD and the GATT and from within the US administration, DC governments seemed set on starving the NICs of markets. Western economists, on the whole, argued that the net effect of trade with the NICs, for Europe at least, was to create jobs, and that where jobs had been lost, as for example in the European textile industry, NIC exports trailed US exports and the introduction of new technology as a contributory factor.[67] Industry interests paid little heed to these academic voices, however. They knew an easy target when they saw one. And once the EEC had procured a new escape clause in the 1977 NFA requirements in the event of severe domestic unemployment or market disruption, it was only a matter of time before the rot spread: geographically, as Canada and the USA, though they had argued against the 'reasonable departure' clause, subsequently claimed the right to use it, and to new sectors, as the cognate EEC demand for unilateral selective safeguards in non-textile trades gradually came to dominate the GATT MTN.[68]

GATT talks came to dominate the North–South dialogue towards the end of 1978, therefore, not simply because of the substantive issues being negotiated, but because the procedure and the timing of the negotiations somehow epitomized the high-handedness of the North. There was another reason, however, and this was that many of the more industrialized LDCs—states such as Brazil, India, or Mexico—now conducted such a substantial two-way trade in manufactured goods with the DCs that they could no longer be suffered as free-riders on the western trade system as in the past, while, for their own part, they now stood to gain more by adherence to the GATT than by continuing to ignore it. This new interdependence of NICs and DCs, much hastened by the relatively rapid growth experienced by the former since 1973, had several consequences. It marked another division between the NICs and the poorest LDCs, which had neither the disposition nor the ability to participate in GATT negotiations. It meant that in this, as in other forums such as UNCLOS, it was becoming a very finely balanced question for the DCs, when faced with unacceptable demands from the Group of 77, whether there was really any future for the option of going it alone with an agreement to which only the DCs were signatories or by forming a club within a club such as the General Agreement to Borrow (GAB) to mitigate the opening up of some formerly

DC-dominated institution, in this case the IMF. Perhaps these larger LDCs were now too important to be ignored? Perhaps they were now in a position, as they had not been before, to hold the DCs to those rather vague assurances of special consideration for the LDCs thrown out at Tokyo in 1973 which would otherwise have been forgotten? But this thought, once voiced, raised in northern minds the question of why, if this were so, they should continue to be indulged by benefiting from the GSP, various GATT exemptions, the IMF CFF, and innumerable other privileges. The *Financial Times* quoted one unnamed western official whose grumpy and patronizing indignation perfectly capture the mood of 1979. 'The treatment given to developing countries in the past', he claimed, 'was similar to that given to children. They were allowed to ignore GATT rules because of their weakness. But they are now growing to be adults and must take on more responsibility'.[69] It was high time that the wealthier LDCs graduated (the word itself indicates the American origins of the concept) by guaranteeing not to raise their already very high tariffs further without consultation and justification, and by starting to take down the high walls surrounding their no longer infant industries.[70] It was indeed already evident from the attention given to the least-developed countries at UNCTAD V and from the developing EEC/ACP relationship embodied in the Lomé Convention that some sort of cleavage between rich and poor LDCs was opening up. What remained uncertain was how far it might represent a dilution of the negotiating solidarity of the Group of 77 or even a deliberate attempt by the DCs to split the South. There was, however, sufficient anxiety on this issue to cloud the one major set of trade negotiations of this period which remains to be considered here, the renegotiation of the Lomé Convention.

Renegotiating the Lomé Convention

Even within the ACP group of countries there was division about the relation of the Lomé Convention to the broader search for a NIEO.[71] The anglophone states, especially the Caribbeans, took Lomé and its renegotiation very seriously as a stepping-stone to the NIEO. Speaking as ACP secretary-general, but representing in fact a sectional view, Percy Patterson of Jamaica publicly proclaimed the need for fundamental changes in the ACP/EEC relationship as negotiations opened in July 1978.[72] So that these sub-global talks should not disturb the unity of the Group of 77 at a critical time, the NIEO hawks in the ACP group wished to delay substantial negotiations until after UNCTAD V in May 1979. Delay would also give a better idea of the extent to which the preferential position of the ACP states, already eroded by the EEC GSP, had been reduced by GATT tariff reductions, and this in turn would assist the ACP states in formulating any necessary compromise on their initial ambitious demand for completely free access to the EEC for all their exports.

When talks did begin in earnest, however, the hawks had a long list of demands which they hoped to see written into a fresh five-year agreement. They were dissatisfied with several aspects of their relations with the EEC, not least the fact that the trade balance between the two groups, which had seen the EEC in deficit in the early 1970s, had now swung quite the other way. Concerning trade, in addition to free access the ACP group wanted a revision of the prevailing rules of origin governing the eligibility of permitted ACP goods for free entry into the EEC. Under Lomé I the rule had been that no less than 50 per cent of the value of eligible goods must have been added within the ACP states taken as a group. But this figure, seemingly generous, still excluded some goods; fish caught in ACP waters by ships largely owned outside the ACP countries would be an example. Moreover the rules were felt to be unnecessarily complicated, constituting a barrier to trade in themselves.

On aid, the radicals demanded the extension of the STABEX system of compensatory finance and an acceleration of the rate of disbursement of STABEX payments, also earmarking of additional aid funds for specific problems, including those of island and land-locked economies, and the freeing of other EEC aid from restrictions so that, in particular, the Caribbeans might divert more of their receipts from this source to purchases in the USA.

By contrast the francophone African states, true to the submissively neo-colonial character of their bilateral relationship with France, preferred to set aside the romanticism and rhetoric of the NIEO and treat the EEC/ACP negotiations as a mundane functional matter; and, as it happened, theirs was the more realistic appraisal of the circumstances prevailing as talks began. This time round the EEC had no reason to embark on the kind of fundamental revision of its relations with the Third World that had been forced on it five years before by British accession. Moreover, the world economy, then booming, was now in recession. Member states were pre-occupied with domestic unemployment and inflation. Within the EEC they were taken up with direct elections to a European Assembly, the conclusion of the Tokyo Round, the creation of a new European Monetary System, and enlargement negotiations with Greece, Spain, and Portugal which promised to complicate considerably EEC trade relations with other more distant associates including the ACP states and adding a further twist to the fiendishly difficult question of CAP reform. Accordingly, the Europeans were inclined to attempt a quick, businesslike renegotiation which would effectively extend Lomé I, without fundamental change, for ten years. The European Commission was consequently sent into the negotiations with a much more tightly drawn mandate than in 1973, and the frequent need of EEC officials to refer back to the Council of Ministers or to individual member governments, being imperfectly understood by ACP negotiators, soon gave rise to a feeling that the Europeans were deliberately taking up an inflexible and highhanded stance.

This was largely true, though it need not have been so publicly and offensively displayed. Certainly the Commission had no friendly initiatives to pull out of the hat when deadlock seemed imminent, nothing as innovatory as the STABEX scheme which it had proposed in 1974. Indeed those initiatives the Commission made on this occasion simply served further to alienate the ACP radicals, and quite fruitlessly, as it turned out, since there was no very firm consensus in favour of them even within the EEC. The Commission enlisted support from Britain and the Netherlands for the idea of a human rights clause making Lomé II aid transfers conditional on the good behaviour of recipient governments.[73] But Britain, with its record in Northern Ireland, was an unfortunate ally to have adopted on this issue, and France was anyway opposed to a principle which might have been used to offend some of its African clients and which led promptly to embarrassing counterdemands for improved status and treatment for North African and other guest-workers living in Europe, of whom there had been almost four million in France at the start of the recession before a somewhat fraudulent repatriation policy was introduced.

A second EEC demand of a not dissimilar kind was for investment guarantees. Here the Europeans took the view that development depended critically upon private direct foreign investment, and that this had been deterred in recent years by heightened political tension, expropriations, and aggressive taxation policies in the ACP states. West Germany, anxious about mineral supplies in the long run, was inclined to link an extension of STABEX to cover copper and other minerals to ACP promises of preferential treatment for European-based multinationals. But the ACP states were extremely wary of this tactic. All opposed the notion of preference for foreigners over local capitalists. More subtly, the Caribbean radicals were anxious not to deter investment by Japanese and US multinationals through appearing to prefer those of the EEC. And here, as in their demand for the untying of EEC aid, the Caribbeans pursued not simply their own regional interest, but the more important principle of third-world unity. The more exclusive the ACP/EEC relationship appeared, the more likely it was to offend other members of the Group of 77. Here, indeed, was a further reason to reject the West German proposal, for it was too evidently part of a broader strategy intended to establish STABEX as a viable *alternative* to the UNCTAD Common Fund, and so detach key mineral exporting countries such as Zambia and Zaïre from the Group of 77 position on the Integrated Programme for Commodities.

Matters were made worse by poor preparatory work from the ACP secretariat, which failed fully to anticipate the intransigence of the EEC and so permitted ACP negotiators to launch themselves headlong into the talks with unrealistically ambitious initial demands. This secretarial weakness was especially damaging for two reasons. It meant that the ACP negotiators showed a rapid rate of concession from the start of the negotiations, encouraging their EEC counterparts to become over-confident and stiffen their own demands.[74] It also meant that, in retreat from their initial positions on broad questions of principle, the ACP states found no adequately prepared arguments with which to extract more modest but substantial concessions on matters of detail where the Europeans might have been more willing to bend. In addition, early exposure of the division between anglophone hawks and francophone doves weakened the ACP position as a whole by letting the EEC identify the relatively small number of states that needed to be bought off by particular concessions or side payments in order to subvert the collective ACP stance.

In October 1978, the asymmetrical character of the EEC/ACP relationship received further confirmation. Amongst other demands put by the EEC to its Associates in the negotiations had been the request that the ACP states submit to obligatory consultation in the event of any threat of disruption of EEC markets arising from ACP exports. But now, with talks under way, came a unilateral announcement of EEC MFA-style quantitative restrictions on imports of textiles from the ACP states. Then in May the following year, with only six months remaining before Lomé I expired, ACP rejection of the EEC aid offer precipitated a complete breakdown of negotiations only overcome the following month by a largely cosmetic 10 per cent increase in the aid package.

The final outcome, agreed at the end of October 1979, showed very little movement from the original EEC position. There was virtually no change in rules of origin, and aid, while higher in nominal terms, represented a decline in real resources per capita from the levels set under Lomé I.[75] There were however a few straws for the ACP states to clutch at. In spite of their considerably weaker negotiating position, not just generally but on this specific issue, the sugar protocol was renewed with little change. The initially provocative EEC stance on human rights was muted; there was a mention in the preamble, but no conditionality of aid transfers. There was also a slight easing in the terms of the STABEX scheme. Yet the only substantial innovation was the creation of a MINEX scheme, extending compensatory finance of a very guarded and limited nature to cover copper, tin, and a handful of other minerals, making provision for EEC emergency aid in the event of disrupted production, and loosely committing the EEC to sponsor minerals joint-ventures in the ACP states, in exchange for which EEC MNCs were assured that future national regulations in the ACP states would treat them no worse than other foreign corporations.

So 1979 drew to a close in an atmosphere of strained East–West relations and deepening OECD recession. LDC hopes that sledge-hammer negotiations within the CIEC or the UN might suddenly release a stream of functional concessions were quiescent. Flagship of UNCTAD, the IPC limped on, rusty and barnacled. Perceptions of a deteriorating international trade regime received repeated confirmation in the Tokyo Round, in MFA II, and in Lomé II. Prophecy had indeed given way to negotiation in UNCTAD and elsewhere, but negotiation in an atmosphere substantially sourer and less conducive to compromise than that which had prevailed in the recent past.

Notes

1. On Angola, Ethiopia, etc., see Arthur Gavshon, *Crisis in Africa: Battle-ground of East and West* (Harmondsworth, Penguin, 1981).
2. *Financial Times*, 25 January and 25 September 1979; and see Gavshon, op. cit., Chapter 8.
3. See Olivier Carré, 'Steps towards Peace' in Maxime Rodinson, *Israel and the Arabs* (Harmondsworth, Penguin, 1982).
4. On Iran see Fred Halliday, *Iran: Dictatorship and Development* (Harmondsworth, Penguin, 1979) and Barry Rubin, *Paved with Good Intentions: the American Experience and Iran* (Harmondsworth, Penguin, 1980).
5. This account owes much to essays by Jonathan Steele and John Gittings in Noam Chomsky *et al.*, *Superpowers in Collision: the New Cold War* (Harmondsworth, Penguin, 1982).
6. Independent Commission on International Development Issues (Chairman, Willy Brandt), *North–South: a programme for survival* (London, Pan, 1980). A number of reviews are listed in note 31, below.
7. Chomsky *et al.*, op. cit., p. 26.

8. I. M. D. Little, 'Distributive Justice and the New International Economic Order', in Peter Oppenheimer, ed., *Issues in International Economics* (London, Routledge & Kegan Paul, 1978), pp. 37–53.

9. Department of Political and Security Council Affairs, *The United Nations and Disarmament, 1970–75* (New York, United Nations, 1975); Ian Smart, 'Janus: the Nuclear God', *The World Today*, 34 (1978), 118–27.

10. Smart, ibid.

11. David P. Calleo and Benjamin M. Rowland, *America and the World Political Economy: Atlantic Dreams and National Realities* (Bloomington, Ind., and London, Indiana University Press, 1973), p. 123, and see Chomsky, op. cit., p. 31.

12. *Financial Times*, 6 February 1978. India was to receive unlimited supplies of crude oil from Iran, the proceeds being left in India in rupees, to be invested in major industrial and agricultural projects. Payment was to be in the form of a share in the output of these projects: grain, alumina, paper products, and iron ore. A similar arrangement was envisaged with Pakistan. The revolution put paid to all this for a time.

13. Consejo Argentino para las Relaciones Internacionales, 'La Argentina y el Proceso de Restructuramiento de la Associación Latinoamericana de Libre Comercio' (Buenos Aires, 1979, mimeo), p. 140, quoted in Diana Tussie, 'Latin American Integration: from LAFTA to LAIA', *Journal of World Trade Law*, 16 (1982), p. 412.

14. Tussie, op. cit., p. 412.

15. 'South–South Dialogue: a Brief Report', *Third World Quarterly*, 1 (1979), 117–22, reports on a meeting of third-world intellectuals, policy-makers, and negotiators, held at Arusha in December 1978.

16. *Guardian*, 11 September 1978; *Financial Times*, 12 and 13 September 1978.

17. *Guardian*, 15 November 1978.

18. On NIC-based MNCs, see Tamir Agmon and C. P. Kindleberger, eds, *Multinationals from Small Countries* (Cambridge, Mass., MIT Press, 1977) and Krishna Kumar and Maxwell G. McLoed, eds, *Multinationals from Developing Countries* (Lexington, Mass., Lexington Books, 1981).

19. See, for example, Shridath S. Ramphal, 'Not by Unity Alone: the case for Third World Organization', *Third World Quarterly*, 1 (1979), 43–52.

20. Richard J. Powers, 'United Nations Voting Alignments: a New Equilibrium', *Western Political Quarterly*, 33 (1980), 167–84, Table 1, pp. 174–8, and see also the interesting if inconclusive study by Douglas C. Smyth, 'The Global Economy and the Third World: coalition or cleavage?', *World Politics*, 29 (1977), 584–603.

21. *Financial Times*, 22 May 1979.

22. *Guardian*, 29 May 1979.

23. *Financial Times*, 13 September 1979.

24. V. M. Nair, 'Havana Summit Shows up Non-Aligned Divisions', *The Round Table*, 227 (1980), 99–101; and see Fouad Ajami, 'The Fate of Non-Alignment', *Foreign Affairs*, 59 (1980/1), 366–85, and Peter Willetts, *The Non-Aligned in Havana* (London, Frances Pinter, 1981).

25. *Guardian*, 16 May 1979.

26. *Financial Times*, 31 August 1979.

27. *Financial Times*, 31 August 1979.

28. *Guardian*, 20 August 1979.

29. R. Krishnamurti, 'UNCTAD as a Negotiating Institution', *Journal of World Trade Law*, 15 (1981), p. 25.

30. Independent Commission on International Development Issues, op. cit., especially pp. 16, 18, 20–1, 22.
31. Reviews of the Brandt Report, some of them no more friendly than this, abound. They include P. D. Henderson, 'Survival, Development and the Report of the Brandt Commission', *The World Economy*, 3 (1980), 87–117; Barbara Ward, 'Another Chance for the North?', *Foreign Affairs*, 59 (1980/81), 386–97; and short papers by P. D. Henderson, Kenneth Minogue, William Letwin, and Elie Kedourie, in *Encounter*, 55 (1980), 12–30, under the general title, 'What's Wrong with the Brandt Report?', together with further discussion in the same journal, 56 (1981), 75–81.
32. Ursula Wassermann, 'The Common Fund', *Journal of World Trade Law*, 11 (1977), 377–9; Geoffrey Goodwin, 'The UNCTAD Common Fund—challenge and response', *The World Today* (November 1977), 425–32. See also H. W. Singer, 'The Common Fund Debate', *The Round Table*, 271 (1978), 229–35.
33. *Financial Times*, 22 February and 17 April 1978; *Guardian*, 17 April 1978.
34. *Financial Times*, 27 November 1978.
35. *Guardian* 1 December 1978; *Financial Times*, 1 December 1978.
36. *Guardian*, 9 April 1979.
37. C. Brown, *The Political and Social Economy of Commodity Control* (London, Macmillan, 1980), p. 168.
38. Ibid., pp. 175–7.
39. Ibid., p. 179.
40. *Financial Times*, 11 December 1979.
41. *Financial Times*, 7 June 1978.
42. *Financial Times*, 7 July 1978.
43. *Financial Times*, 5 December 1980.
44. *Financial Times*, 16 December 1977; *Guardian*, 27 February 1978.
45. *Financial Times*, 3 August 1978; *Guardian*, 20 November 1978.
46. *Guardian*, 26 November 1979.
47. *Financial Times*, 14 November 1979.
48. Quoted in *Financial Times*, 5 July 1979.
49. *Financial Times*, 4 December 1979.
50. *Financial Times*, 30 January 1979.
51. *Guardian*, 11 September 1978.
52. *Financial Times*, 12 December 1978.
53. *Financial Times*, 10 April 1979.
54. *Financial Times*, 28 February 1978.
55. Robert L. Curry Jr, 'Africa's External Debt Situation', *Journal of Modern African Studies*, 17 (1979), pp. 16, *et seq.*
56. *Guardian*, 17 December 1977, 4 and 14 March, 12 June, 19 July, 1 August, and 11 October 1978 and 7 May 1979. *Financial Times*, 27 and 28 February, 1 August 1978.
57. Anila Graham, 'The Transfer of Technology: Test Case in the North–South Dialogue: a Historical Review', *Journal of International Affairs*, 33 (1979), 1–17.
58. Constantin Vaitsos, quoted in V. N. Balasubramanyam, 'Transfer of Technology: the UNCTAD Arguments in Perspective', *The World Economy*, I (1977), 69–80, puts it neatly: 'The item itself that one needs to purchase is at the same time the information that is needed in order to make a rational decision to buy it'.

59. *Guardian*, 9 October 1978 (Surendra J. Patel). Balasubramanyam, op. cit., provides a cogent critique of UNCTAD arguments on the transfer and alleged overpricing of technology.
60. S. Joekes and C. H. Kirkpatrick, 'The Results of UNCTAD V', *Journal of World Trade Law*, 13 (1979), p. 542.
61. Victoria Curzon Price, 'Surplus Capacity and What the Tokyo Round Failed to Settle', *The World Economy*, 2 (1979), 305-18.
62. *Guardian*, 21 September and 18 and 20 November 1978; *Financial Times*, 30 November 1978.
63. *Financial Times*, 23 March 1979.
64. *Financial Times*, 4 April 1979.
65. *Financial Times*, 20 April, 2 and 3 May 1979.
66. *Financial Times*, 1 July 1980.
67. *Guardian*, 25 May 1978, 19 May 1980, 20 May 1981; *Financial Times*, 18 January 1979.
68. *Financial Times*, 3 May 1979.
69. *Financial Times*, 14 May 1979.
70. For further discussion of this question see Isaiah Frank, 'The "Graduation" Issue for LDCs', *Journal of World Trade Law*, 13 (1979), 289-302.
71. This section draws principally on John Ravenhill, 'Asymmetrical Interdependence: Renegotiating the Lomé Convention', *International Journal*, 35 (1979/80), 150-69; Carol Cosgrove Twitchett, 'Towards a New ACP-EC Convention', *The World Today* (December 1978); and Adrian Hewitt and Christopher Stevens, 'The Second Lomé Convention', in Christopher Stevens, ed., *EEC and the Third World: a Survey*, I (London, Hodder & Stoughton Ltd., 1981), pp. 30-59.
72. *Guardian*, 10 July 1978.
73. *Financial Times*, 27 January and 17 February 1978.
74. The assumption that rapid concession encourages further demands is argued for by Ravenhill, 'Asymmetrical Interdependence', p. 163, citing I. William Zartman, 'The Analysis of Negotiation', in I. W. Zartman, ed., *The 50% Solution*, and John G. Cross, *The Economics of Bargaining* (New York, Basic Books, 1969).
75. Hewitt and Stevens, pp. 52-3.

The purpose of this final chapter is twofold. A brief survey of the state of negotiations within the UN system, the GATT and the IMF is followed by a general conclusion assessing some of the abiding themes of the North–South dialogue over the past decade.

Global Negotiations, Cancún, and the Politicization
of the UN System

Within the UN family of organizations, functional negotiations on commodities, shipping, the transfer of technology, the problem of the least-developed countries, the law of the sea, the allocation of radio frequencies, and a new information and communications order have continued since 1979 at their customary slow pace, and, as before, have frequently been dominated by North–South disagreements. At the same time attempts have continued in the General Assembly to reach agreement to hold Global Negotiations which would seek to break deadlocks elsewhere. Preparatory meetings of the Committee of the Whole in March, May, and July 1980 led on to a stalemate in the UN Special Session which took place in September 1980, effectively delaying the Global Negotiations which had been planned for 1981.

In the meantime a rival forum for all-embracing negotiations was being formed. The Brandt Report had appealed for a summit conference of selected world leaders as the most likely way of injecting new dynamism into the sluggish dialogue between rich and poor states. In May 1980, after a meeting with Brandt and Chancellor Kreisky of Austria in Bonn, President López Portillo of Mexico agreed to host such a meeting. Originally intended for a date early in 1981, the summit had to be postponed while the new United States administration took stock and ultimately unsuccessful Austrian attempts to secure Soviet participation ran their course. Eventually twenty-two heads of state met at Cancún, on the Mexican coast, in October 1981 under the joint chairmanship of López Portillo and Prime Minister Trudeau of Canada.

The outcome was insubstantial and disappointing. No major initiatives were announced; indeed no firm decisions were taken at all. The group refused to institutionalize itself into a club, meeting periodically to survey the state of North–South relations. The Mexicans had listed a number of demands in the preparatory meetings, seeking a new IMF compensatory finance facility for food-importing LDCs, curbs on DC protectionism, extension of GSPs, a greater role for official international institutions in the determination of world liquidity, more LDC control over the IMF and the World Bank, a relative as well as absolute increase in the IMF quotas of LDCs, and DC commitment to aid targets. None of these proposals was new. Most were being actively pursued elsewhere. None of the major northern states saw any reason for concession. Moreover many of the leading southern states had reason to be content with failure at Cancún. The Algerians, as chief protagonists in the parallel moves to establish Global Negotiations within the UN were alive to the threat posed to those negotiations by any revival of the belief that a selective, CIEC-like forum was to be preferred because less cumbersome and rigid than the UN. Bangladesh, as the next to take the chair in the General Assembly, and Venezuela, currently in the chair at the Group of 77, were equally concerned to avoid any appearance of betraying the broad interest of the South. In the end it was agreed that Global Negotiations in the UN ought indeed to go forward, though not what they would comprise. President Reagan spoke a good deal of the virtues of the free market and offered a team of flying farmers to advise on agricultural problems in the Third World. The meeting broke up with all participants agreed that it had been a success, and observers equally unanimous in their verdicts of failure.

But if that elusive substance, political will, could not easily be directed toward the benevolent invigoration of international organizations, it was far from absent from their deliberations. More and more the official United States view was that extraneous politicization was precluding much-needed technical agreement in one functional area after another, to the point where the UN system ceased to be either useful or true to its original principle of universality. After the Israeli bombing of an IAEA-supervised Iraqi nuclear reactor, the Reagan administration reacted with particular vigour to attempts to exclude Israel from the International Telecommunications Union, the IAEA itself, and other UN bodies during 1981 and 1982, withdrawing its own delegates, stopping payments and even threatening to leave the UN altogether.[1] The United States was angered and alarmed also by its failure to exclude pro-Soviet Nicaragua from a place on the UN Security Council in October 1982. Opposition to US policy in Central America appeared to have destroyed the slender majority which the State Department had succeeded in orchestrating to keep Cuba off the Council two years before.[2] And similar Group B anger was aroused by attempts to exclude South Africa from the

Universal Postal Union and WIPO in 1979 and to allow the PLO to participate in the Treaty on the Law of the Sea.[3]

Primary Commodities

In spite of these distractions negotiations have proceeded within UNCTAD and elsewhere in recent years. Yet the central role of UNCTAD in the quest for an NIEO had been increasingly questioned. By the end of 1979 the powerful Arab oil-exporting states were showing signs of preferring the General Assembly to UNCTAD as a platform for resounding speeches linking energy and development issues to Middle East security questions.[4] This had been reflected in the creation of the Committee of the Whole and the pressure for Global Negotiations, and had arisen partly because the very success of UNCTAD in moving from prophecy to negotiation had dispersed its charisma.

What remained were the tedious final stages of negotiation and ratification of initiatives dating back to the mid-1970s. The Common Fund, for example, went for ratification in June 1980, on the understanding that it would start operating as soon as ninety states representing a minimum of 66 per cent of the intended $470 million capital had confirmed their support. It soon became apparent that ratification would be no mere formality. In October 1980, at talks in Geneva on the rules to govern the operation of the Common Fund, delegates failed even to adopt rules of procedure for their own deliberations.[5] By May 1981, almost a year after agreement had finally been reached, only thirty-four states representing 57 per cent of the Fund's capital had signed, while Indonesia alone had ratified. Vital details such as the precise form of agreement to link ICAs to the Fund were still under negotiation late in 1981, and by February 1982 the number of ratifications still stood well short of the target.[6] With a deadline of 31 March rapidly approaching, only twenty-one states had ratified, seven of these being DCs. UNCTAD officials watched in despair as the major Latin American exporters of primary commodities stood aloof. Producer jubilation at the apparently generous share of voting power in the Fund's governing council given to the Group of 77 countries turned out to have been premature. The sting in the tail was that direct contributors— whether developed or less developed—received ten times as many votes for each dollar deposited as did producer countries contributing indirectly through ICAs depositing with the Fund.[7]

There were other reasons, too, why many producers hung back. In part, it was simply that UNCTAD had succeeded too well. It had returned, dog-like, with the offensive and decaying bone which the more sophisticated and wealthier members of the Group of 77 had thought irretrievable. After years of urging UNCTAD to greater efforts they had now to admit that they had been bluffing in an effort to preserve the unity of the Group of 77 for purposes of their own.

Specifically, exporters of several key commodities had come to the view that affiliation to the Fund would not serve their interests, while the weak level of demand for commodities, exacerbated by aggressive US postures in international negotiations, had caused considerable resentment and disillusion with ICAs in general.

UNCTAD officials had certainly scored a modest success by halting the trend evident in 1979 towards independent producer action over cocoa. The International Cocoa Agreement was indeed abrogated at the end of March 1980, and Carlos Alberto Andrado Pinto, a veteran of the Brazilian Coffee Institute, took over the Cocoa Producers' Alliance with a mandate to stabilize the market independently around a price of $150 per lb.[8] But as prices moved remorselessly down UNCTAD officials succeeded in organizing fresh talks between consumers and producers for October and delaying the division of the old International Cocoa Organization buffer-stock fund. During the negotiations, the US delegation fought successfully for an agreement based primarily on a buffer stock and resolutely opposed export controls. But having played a major part in shaping the new agreement the US then failed to join because its representatives rightly considered the floor price of 110 cents per lb. unrealistically high. At the same time the biggest producer, the Ivory Coast, stayed out of the pact, though for quite different reasons. In a weak market the new buffer-stock fund was exhausted in a matter of weeks early in 1982, much as United States and British officials had expected. Thus cocoa remained governed by the sort of agreement which could in principle affiliate to a Common Fund. (Indeed the slack market during 1982 offered a perfect example of the circumstances in which the Common Fund might be able to assist an ICA.) Yet the agreement was seriously flawed, because the political process of arithmetically splitting the difference between opposed negotiating positions had produced inadequate means of stabilization for the agreed price range. The lesson for UNCTAD was that it would take only one or two such agreements at a time of slack global demand to exhaust the resources of a Common Fund, substantial though these might be, unless it were very tightly and conservatively managed.

The same US opposition to quantitative controls on exports was evident in negotiations for the sixth International Tin Agreement

(ITA) in the first half of 1981. These negotiations remained quite independent of UNCTAD, of course, and producers had already made clear their opposition to any link with the Common Fund. Nevertheless the recent history of the ITA is of relevance to the IPC because it helps explain a more general southern disillusion with ICAs and with current United States attitudes.

As in the 1980 cocoa talks, so in the 1981 tin discussions, US representatives opposed export controls as a means of stabilizing prices, insisting on a buffer stock. But by March 1981 the US negotiators were expressing doubt about the need for any ITA at all, to the anger even of such usually moderate producers as the Australians.[9] Finally agreement was reached in June without the USA. However this was rapidly followed by manoeuvres outside the ITA framework as an unidentified buying syndicate, thought ultimately to be under the control of the Malaysian government, began to drive prices up, while the US government responded by opening up its formerly domestic sales from the strategic stockpile to non-US buyers.

The year 1982 found the Malaysians in militant mood, intent on cajoling their reluctant neighbours into an effective producer organization that could use export quotas as well as a buffer stock to control the market should the sixth ITA fail to come into operation or prove inadequate at the end of the year.[10] The wisdom of the Malaysian position was evident during the closing months of 1982 as International Tin Council stocking had to be complemented by export quota cuts of more than one-third to hold the fifth ITA floor price.

These events undoubtedly influenced the behaviour of rubber exporting states, several of which were also major tin producers. Rubber had been the brightest prospect of the IPC in 1979 as agreement was reached on a pact which, in accordance with US wishes, stressed the buffer stock to the exclusion of export controls. Though they had finally stayed out of the cocoa and tin agreements in spite of their considerable influence on the negotiations, the Americans actually ratified the new rubber agreement in October 1980. The administration was embarrassed, however, by a severe cut made by Congress in the US contribution to buffer-stock funds; and the political cost of this, and of US behaviour in other commodity negotiations, became evident as rubber prices weakened further from the thirty-year high of 1979 during 1981. For it was soon evident that Malaysia and some other major producers felt the rubber agreement price-band to be inadequate, and were prepared to act independently of the consumer states through the ANRPC to hold back production in order to defend a price above the floor of 150 Malaysian cents per kilo.[11] The closing weeks of 1982 also saw dissent within the International Natural Rubber Organization (INRO) as West Germany took exception to what it felt to be a too rapid rate of purchase by the buffer-stock manager while the price still remained in the band between 167 and 177 Malaysian cents per kilo in which purchase was optional, not compulsory.[12] The Germans plainly felt that INRO was being misused to support a higher average price than the market justified. The Malaysians, by contrast, were pressing for a more consistent and supportive buying policy from INRO while continuing at the same time, in tandem with their efforts in the tin market, to secure the support of the reluctant Thais and other producers for independent ANRPC action.[13]

The remaining ICAs, covering sugar and coffee, continued to operate by export quotas rather than buffer stocks. Towards the end of 1981, sugar fell below the ISA floor in spite of maximum quota cuts as the EEC free-rode to a production level for that year more than six times higher than its 1973–7 annual average. It was evident that no serious stabilization was to be looked for without the co-operation of the EEC, and ISO–EEC talks on the possible stocking of EEC sugar began in October 1982 ahead of negotiations for a new ISA planned for May 1983. The Coffee Agreement, like the ISA, proved unable to halt the 1981 fall as the floor price was passed in June. A new pact agreed in September 1982, like its predecessor, was based on export quotas rather than a buffer stock. In the meantime, United States pressure had persuaded the producers to abandon their independent attempts to manipulate coffee prices through Pan Café, the executive arm of the Bogotá Group, late in 1980.

It is hard to look back over these recent events without sympathizing with the United States view that only very large buffer stocks defending modest floor prices can hope to survive in a world recession. US objection to the use of export controls to supplement buffer-stock arrangements have rested upon the fear that withholding of supplies could be used by producers to raise prices above trend, so triggering upward adjustments of the price band to be defended by buffer-stock managers, and there plainly need to be some provisions for the adjustment of price ranges if ICAs are not to risk being left entirely behind by the market. This reasonable objection to mixed ICAs leaves open the quotas-only style of ICA currently governing sugar and coffee, and though these are subject to endless argument about the distribution of quotas and are felt by consumers to place unnecessary constraints on supply, they do seem to have found favour with producers in a period of deep recession, as recent Malaysian policy has shown. However, they offer nothing to a Common Fund, leaving UNCTAD in an unenviable position, unable to abandon the principle of buffer stocking, yet unable to accept the full financial demands of such a system and unwilling to admit publicly to the sheer impracticability of employing it to maintain prices even a shade above trend in the long run. In these circumstances the future of the Common Fund appears anything but assured.

Shipping

One natural response of UNCTAD to these discouraging signs in the commodity markets has been to press on with more promising ventures such as its various initiatives on shipping, stirred into life after five sleepy years by EEC ratification of the 1974 Code of Conduct for Liner Conferences in 1979. The most controversial aspect of the Code had been its cargo-sharing clause, whereby 80 per cent of cargoes passing between any two states was to be reserved in equal shares for their national fleets, while only 20 per cent would remain available to cross-haulers such as Britain, Denmark, and Greece. The EEC now ratified with this proviso: that the cargo-sharing clause should apply only to trade between EEC and non-OECD states, being in effect, a very convoluted aid measure. Moreover, it remained to be seen how the code, which still lacked US and Japanese support, would operate in practice. Would LDCs establish their own, almost certainly obsolescent and inefficient fleets, or would they simply put their 40 per cent shares in liner traffic out to tender, employing existing major DC operators with the latest technology and using the code to justify stiff licence fees calculated to narrow owners' profit margins?

Whatever might prove to be the practical effect of the Liner Code, its immediate tactical importance was to stimulate demands for a similar code with cargo-sharing provisions to govern bulk transport. Though it threatened to make the residual spot-market risky to the point where investment was deterred and services became erratic because independent ship-owners were unable to hedge their spot-market risks by longer-term charters, the infant Bulk-Shipping Code being spoken of within UNCTAD after 1979 attracted considerable support within the Group of 77.[14]

But the most significant *démarche* of the new decade was to be UNCTAD's declaration of war against the open register or flags of convenience system (ORS). Under the ORS a growing proportion of the tonnage belonging to major DC-based extractive MNCs and specialist ship-owners had been registered in Liberia, Panama, and three other third-world states providing lax safety and labour regulations and levying very modest taxes. UNCTAD officials have argued that abolition of open registers would raise the costs of the multinationals and so enable LDCs to compete effectively at last and raise their proportion of world tonnage to something more in line with their percentage of world cargoes, so substantially increasing total third-world freight revenues and helping to make it possible for the cargo-sharing provisions of the Liner Code and any future bulk-shipping code to be put into effect. Existing open-register states argue that abolition of the system will lead many owners to domicile their companies and register their ships with cheap-labour northern maritime nations, chiefly Greece and Britain, rather than invest in LDCs such as Argentina, Brazil, or India. Prospective open-register states such as Sri Lanka and Nigeria are also sceptical, and outright opposition is to be anticipated from LDCs such as the Philippines, with a vested interest in remittances from sailors employed on ORS ships, since the UNCTAD proposals would almost certainly disturb their dominance.

In short, the attack on open registries has so far met with opposition from a vociferous minority of the Group of 77 and the major maritime states, indifference from many least-developed and landlocked states in the Third World, and support from the seamen's trade unions in the North and the dozen or so LDCs in Latin America, the Middle East, and Asia with national fleets of some size.[15] Small wonder that preparatory negotiations in May 1982 ended without agreement while further talks at inter-governmental working group level in November of the same year seemed unlikely to produce an agreed text to go forward to the planned 1983 final conference.[16]

The Transfer of Technology

Shipping had the great advantage for UNCTAD of being an issue on which overlaps with other international organizations were slight, so countering by now traditional northern accusations of redundancy. The regulation of MNCs and the transfer of technology were quite the reverse. The EEC, the OECD, ANCOM, and numerous UN agencies aside from UNCTAD had pitched in with codes, while innovative national laws with international implications concerning taxation, competition, transfer pricing, and other relevant issues had been passed by individual states, both North and South, during the

1970s. Amid this welter of regulation there could, however, be discerned a Group of 77 view, preferring legally binding codes, strong national regulation, and the settlement of disputes in the courts of the host state, and demanding rapid transfer of technology as well. This package continues to be pushed simultaneously in a number of forums, of which UNCTAD is only one, in the hope that the procedures, political environment, and timing of at least one will eventually yield substantial results.

Setting aside the obvious relevance of UNCTAD's shipping proposals to extractive and shipping MNCs and the perennial but growing southern stress on the transfer of civil nuclear technology in the IAEA, at least four global or near-global organizations have witnessed interesting developments in this sphere during recent years. First came the UN Conference on Science and Technology for Development (UNCSTD), held in Vienna in August 1979. The already familiar demand for a more just share of the world's technology was voiced by the Group of 77, and it was proposed that a new body funded by contributions in the region of $1 billion a year from the DCs should be set up to foster research and technological development in the LDCs. Not unexpectedly, this demand for a new institution met with little enthusiasm from the DCs; it appeared too obviously to overlap with existing agencies.[17]

Accordingly, the Group of 77 took away their demand, refurbished it at their ministerial meeting in Havana during December 1979, and wheeled it out again at UNIDO III in New Delhi early the next year.[18] At its second full meeting, in the heady atmosphere of 1975, the United Nations Industrial Development Organization (UNIDO) had adopted an ambitious programme, setting the target of a much increased third-world share in total industrial output by the end of the century. It now met to discuss a series of proposals, none of which was uniquely its own and all of which had implications for the world's MNCs. The demand for an Industrial Finance Agency to promote industrial and technical co-operation between LDCs which had already been fielded in the UNCSTD the previous year was once again totally rejected by Group B in its new guise; the demand for a new international industrial development law commission clearly trod on the toes of the existing UN Commission on International Trade Law; finally the call for an international patent centre was a transparent attempt to move the vital revision of the 1883 Paris Convention on Patents out of the World Intellectual Property Organization (WIPO) into a more malleable, southern-dominated forum.

Some commentators had indeed suspected that the Group of 77 attack on South Africa during the tenth session of WIPO in

September 1979 and procedural wrangles in the February 1980 session of the same body had served an ulterior purpose, paralysing the traditional forum for discussion of patent law so as to clear the way for UNIDO to set up a rival, southern-dominated patent organization.[19] However, the arguments in the February WIPO meeting were not simply delaying tactics. In part they concerned voting procedure, and would indeed determine whether WIPO could be made into a satisfactory channel for reform or would remain under northern control. The Group of 77 had proposed that, failing consensus on a revised convention, a two-thirds majority be required. This would ensure a built-in majority for the Group of 77 and Group D acting together. The final compromise on voting procedure was rather different. Consensus was preferred, but, should it be unobtainable, revision was to be carried through by a majority vote so long as no more than twelve states objected.

What were the substantive changes which the South sought to secure by determining WIPO procedure? The most important was the principle, central to clause 5A of the revised draft, that companies obtaining patents in foreign countries to protect products or processes must exploit those patents *in the state granting the patent* and not by exports, or else see local rivals authorized to exploit these unutilized innovations under non-voluntary licences. LDCs hoped that a new convention incorporating this clause would encourage investment by firms in the pharmaceuticals and chemical industries, so speeding up the transfer of advanced technology to the South. DCs objected that it would reduce economies of scale in these industries and act as a disincentive to investment. Some progress towards a compromise appeared to take place during 1980 and 1981, with the Group of 77 seeming to accept the idea of transitional privileges limited to twenty-five years and the DCs coming closer to acceptance of the exclusive non-voluntary licence, which would give a local operator, once authorized, a few years to get established before the original holder of the patent could belatedly start exploiting it. By the end of 1981 a compromise draft worked out by F. Jiménez Dávila of Argentina stood ready for final agreement at a meeting scheduled for November 1982, but it seemed unlikely in the extreme that the Reagan administration would accept the compromise, or that second rank DCs such as Australia, Spain, Turkey, or Canada would accept a package that did not give them privileges similar to those sought by the LDCs.[20]

If WIPO was heading towards an impasse, so too was the UNCTAD Code of Conduct on the Transfer of Technology, which was intended to complement and reinforce the demands of the Group of 77 in the

UNCSTD, UNIDO, and WIPO. Here again, the position by the end of 1981 was of superficial compromise. The April 1981 draft included a number of important principles: that all nations had the right to benefit from technological progress, though technology was *not*, as the Group of 77 had urged, the common heritage of mankind; that it was necessary to strengthen the technological capabilities of all states; and that this endeavour required the co-operation of developed and less-developed states. At the same time considerable disagreements still needed to be resolved. The DCs wished to place strict limits on the Code. It should apply only to international transfers, *not* to the transfer of technology from a subsidiary of a DC MNC located in an LDC to a local firm in the same state. It should take the form of a set of guidelines, rather than the more formal convention preferred by the Group of 77.[21]

Yet even an agreement on these lines, falling well short of Group of 77 demands, seemed unlikely to attract United States support were it to be finally adopted by the UN General Assembly in 1983, and the Group of 77 remained divided about the wisdom of accepting a much weakened and toothless compromise.

UNCLOS

Like so many other sets of North–South negotiations, UNCLOS had come to depend more and more on the attitude of the United States since the hostile reaction of the administration to the informal composite negotiating text back in 1977. By 1979 the US government had so despaired of a satisfactory outcome from UNCLOS that it had drafted national legislation on seabed mining in an attempt to provide private consortia with a measure of certainty concerning the legal environment they would encounter as the prospect of large-scale operations drew closer.

In dispute were a whole series of technical and financial issues. How large a payment would consortia have to make to cover the ISA's investigation of its bona fides? Ought a further payment to be made on signature of a contract between a consortium and the ISA, and if so, how large ought this to be? Would mining ventures of long maturation be able to support these front-end charges and the further $1 million a year demanded by the Group of 77 to ensure diligent exploitation of concessions, once awarded? Ought the consortia to make payments to the ISA on the basis of production or profits or some combination of the two, and how was the percentage of profits deriving from the nodules themselves to be distinguished from the percentage of profits contributed by transport and processing activities quite outside the compass of the ISA?[22] All these details had to be negotiated in an atmosphere of massive uncertainty about costs if the DC consortia were to avoid negotiation under pressure, once mining had already started, with an ISA dominated by third-world states including land-based producers of minerals that might seek to control levels of production or milk the consortia dry. To US firms with major interests in seabed consortia such as Kennecott, US Steel, and Lockheed, the best course appeared to be neither advance negotiation of an international regime, nor later submission to an unsympathetic ISA, but unilateral legislation by friendly parent states.

By June 1980, President Carter had succeeded in steering through Congress national legislation that would calm some of these corporate fears by permitting deep-sea mining from 1988.[23] Then, as what many thought would be the final session of UNCLOS III convened in March 1981, the new Reagan administration insisted on delay, backing off from the compromises made by its two predecessors and dismissing the entire US negotiating team.[24] What caused most offence was less the decision to review policy, natural enough for a new government, than the aggressive style of its announcement and the timing, which precluded postponement of the UNCLOS meeting. More than this, perhaps, the South had cause to be disturbed because the Reagan administration, far from being pushed into obstruction by particular pressure from mining consortia opposed to the treaty, had plainly chosen to respond to this pressure in preference to equally strong appeals from US oil companies and senior officers in the armed forces, all concerned to secure the unimpeded passage of shipping promised by the treaty. The only plausible reason for such a step at such a time was that Reagan wished to affirm the ultimate power of the United States as the largest national economy in the world to make a nonsense of the painstaking work of functional bodies in the UN, so forcibly reminding the South that reform, unlike revolution, depends finally on the consent of the powerful.

Not until the beginning of 1982 did the USA return to the UNCLOS negotiations with the lordly demand that while other parts of the treaty were left untouched, the deep-seabed regime be modified substantially in order to assure US consortia of access to the seabed, to safeguard them against transfer of technology requirements and unreasonable financial demands, and to give the US government greater power within the ISA and a veto on amendments to the treaty once in force.[25] All of these were, of course, matters on which delegates had already deliberated and compromised at earlier sessions of UNCLOS, and their resurrection as a set of unilateral demands was deeply frustrating to other participant states, the more so when it was backed up by a US attempt to secure a rival interim treaty on the law of the sea between major OECD states including Britain and France.[26]

In spite of LDC resentment at US high-handedness, discussion of the US proposals proceeded during April 1982, but at the end of the month delegates voted to accept the completed treaty, finally abandoning the principle of consensus which had been adopted at the outset of the negotiations eight years before. While 130 of the 151 states represented voted for the treaty, seventeen (mostly European states) abstained, and four, including the USA, opposed.[27] The US appeared finally to have decided that it could have the benefits of a law of the sea treaty without entering into potentially costly commitments, reasoning that the rights of passage through territorial waters so vital to US trade and strategic interests would in all probability be assured by customary international law, and that, in any case, the US could free-ride on a law of the sea treaty guaranteeing these rights even if it were not itself a signatory. The Group of 77, for its part, had proved willing to put at risk the fruits of years of negotiation by insisting, to the very end, on the right of the PLO to sign the final act of the conference.[28]

Since April 1982 other DCs, including Britain and West Germany, have expressed their intention to delay signing, let alone ratifying the treaty, in the hope that concessions may yet be made to the US deep-seabed regime demands. The prospect of further negotiations is not, however, to be taken entirely seriously since it is apparent that while the seabed regime has provided the pretext for the tough policy of Reagan and his allies, the most fundamental United States objection is an ideologically motivated aversion to the principle of community on which the regime is based rather than its financial and constitutional details, and that principle of community will not lightly be abandoned by the Group of 77.

World Trade and the GATT

It was perhaps unfortunate that western leaders meeting in Ottawa at their 1981 economic summit should have proposed a fresh ministerial meeting of the GATT signatories, the first since Tokyo in 1973. Their intention, no doubt, was to create a platform for endorsement of the value of the liberal trading order and condemnation of protectionism; but as preparatory talks between officials in

Geneva proceeded during the European Summer of 1982 it became apparent that the OECD leaders had opened up a can of worms.

No major states wished to embark on a full round of MTNs so soon after the conclusion of the Tokyo Round, especially since the domestic climate was extremely protectionist on both sides of the Atlantic, and therefore unlikely to yield the sort of mandate that would make protracted talks worthwhile. The effect of the ministerial meeting was therefore to expose publicly the extent of the breakdown of international agreement on a variety of trade questions, and to open up wounds barely healed since the Tokyo Round by further discussion of the legitimacy of selective import controls, the definition of export subsidies, the extension of the GATT to embrace services and agricultural goods, and the concept of graduation of NICs such as Brazil from GSP to less privileged status.

The ministerial meeting, held in November 1982, took place against a background of growing dispute in trade relations between the USA and the EEC and between both of these major northern participants in world trade and their principal southern partners.

The Tokyo Round had scarcely been concluded when US–EEC trade relations took a turn for the worse. Disputes flared up over steel, farm products, and a range of petrochemicals-based products including fertilizers and textiles, and the bundle of trade disputes dividing the major NATO allies became even more heavily politicized as the Reagan administration weighed in with a clumsy and ultimately unsuccessful attempt to isolate the Soviet Union by suspending western participation in a new pipeline project. To assign responsibility in any of these disputes is difficult because, beneath the political postures, there are real technical complexities; and if the dispute selected for more detailed treatment here is that which shows the EEC in the least unfavourable light it must at once be said that this is coincidental, and that the choice is determined solely by its particular relevance to EEC trade relations with the Third World. For it is certainly the case that the failure of the EEC textile lobby to get satisfaction in dealings with the USA has made it much more hawkish than it might otherwise have been in its attitudes towards the NICs in MFA talks.

The trouble may be traced back to EEC dissatisfaction with the deal struck in the GATT MTN on textile tariffs. The strength of the textile lobby in the USA had been such that the Carter administration had failed to get through Congress textiles concessions of the same magnitude as those offered by the EEC.[29] European discontent with what was felt to be a lopsided settlement increased markedly during 1979 as US exports of synthetic fibres to the EEC began to rise markedly, pushing up the US market share for these products in the UK and Italy by more than 400 per cent over the previous year.[30] The air was thick with allegations that US manufactures were benefitting unfairly from a concealed export subsidy, being able to buy gas and petroleum at regulated—that is to say subsidized—prices. This affected not simply their energy costs but, much more significantly, their raw material costs, since petroleum or gas were important in the production of ammonia, acetic acid, vinyl acetate monomer, and a wide range of chemicals employed in the synthetic textiles, fertilizers, plastics, and paints industries.[31]

Textile manufacturers wanted the imposition of countervailing duties against the USA. The EEC, anxious about a complementary dispute with the USA concerning steel, where its own exports were threatened with US CVDs, wished to proceed circumspectly. It was all too easy, therefore, for the European Commission to mollify the vociferous textile lobby by taking a tough line in negotiations over the extension of the MFA, even though the surge of imports from the USA was of overwhelmingly greater significance for EEC employment.

MFA II was due to expire at the end of 1981. As before, negotiations were dominated by the EEC, as far and away the largest importer. But this was an EEC in even less generous mood than five years before, intent on pegging overall growth of imports under the MFA at a level of about one per cent while simultaneously shifting national quotas to favour smaller, late-coming exporters at the expense of major NICs such as South Korea, Hong Kong, Brazil, and India. This transparent EEC ploy, presented as a way of assisting the weaker LDCs, looked very much like an attempt to limit imports by giving these states quotas which they could not fulfill. In addition, the EEC was determined to retain the reasonable departures clause incorporated into the MFA in 1977 and to persuade some of the wealthier NICs, notably Brazil, to reduce their own very high tariffs on textiles.[32] The EEC also wanted a recession clause allowing for a review of the agreement should the condition of the European industry deteriorate still further, and a surge mechanism to stop disruption arising from any sudden utilization of previously under-utilized quotas.[33]

This tough negotiating position met with little favour among the NICs, and although a third MFA was formally agreed by consensus within the textiles committee of the GATT on 22 December 1981, a number of NICs remained adamant in their opposition to the terms of bilateral deals offered to them by the EEC, while the EEC made clear that its ratification of the MFA would depend on the conclusion of the bilateral pacts.[34] Acrimonious discussions continued thoughout 1982 as a hard core of NICs, including Hong Kong, South Korea, India, Brazil and Malaysia continued to refuse to sign the MFA or reach bilateral deals until the MFA had been improved.[35]

It has been argued that the intransigence of the EEC in these negotiations owed something to the strength of the European textile lobby, and to the need felt by officials and politicians to provide the industry with some compensation for the beating it was taking from US competitors. However, as NIC resistance to the new MFA continued, this side-show threatened to move to the central stage and upset yet another aspect of the complicated US–EEC trade relationship. By August 1982 it was apparent that if the MFA talks collapsed and the EEC withdrew from the arrangement, it would meet the demand of its manufacturers by imposing selective safeguards unilaterally, so breaching the important nineteenth article of the GATT which it had so long and so unsuccessfully sought to amend in the face of determined US opposition.

At this point, the solidarity of the intransigent NICs began to break down. India, Colombia, and Yugoslavia concluded bilateral agreements with the EEC in September 1982, only two months ahead of the GATT ministerial talks. Malaysia followed in November.[36] Finally, Hong Kong, the most adamant of the NICs, agreed a compromise with the EEC, submitting to cuts of between 6 and 8 per cent in its quotas of T-shirts, sweaters, trousers, blouses, and shirts, all of them euphemistically termed 'sensitive' items by the EEC.[37]

EEC wrangles with the NICS were mirrored by US squabbles with, amongst others, China and Brazil. After long discussions paralleling those of the EEC with the MFA exporters, the United States finally resorted to the imposition of unilateral restrictions against Chinese textiles early in 1983, in defiance of the GATT.[38] By September 1982 seven legal suits calling for CVDs against Brazilian exports of manufactured and agricultural goods were pending in the US, and the element of political discretion governing continued Brazilian access to this, its leading foreign market, at a time when the country was virtually bankrupt, opened up the Brazilian government to extremely powerful United States pressures for changes in commercial, economic, military, and foreign policies.[39]

The dilemma in which the Brazilians and other populous NICs found themselves was made the more problematic as the GATT ministerial conference of November 1982 drew to a close with a predictably half-hearted condemnation of protectionism, virtually shelving most major questions by instituting further studies and discussions.[40] To the extent that deterioration of the GATT regime inhibited North–South trade it seemed bound to cause further DC unemployment by curbing southern purchasing-power, so further reinforcing northern protectionist sentiment. At the same time, continued recession and low demand threatened the faltering ability of the NICs to service their debts to the major western banks; many were indeed already in virtual default, though this was discreetly masked behind euphemistic pronouncements about rescheduling. To the extent that dilapidation of the liberal order inhibited international trade within the OECD—and 1982 had witnessed serious talk of explicit restrictions even on intra-EEC trade—it seemed likely to further exacerbate existing disagreements between the USA and its allies, and so create mounting pressure within the leading DCs for a more bilateralist pattern of trade and, ultimately, of political relations. This in turn, threatened to restrict the diplomatic freedom of action which LDCs had come to enjoy during the 1970s, when division in the North, while offering opportunities for southern diplomacy, had never been allowed to get out of hand.

Would the unity of the Group of 77 survive exclusive recruitment drives for clients and allies in the Third World by the USA, the EEC, and Japan? Would individual states in the Third World be able to resist the pressures to submit to neo-colonial relationships, when the alternative might be economic disaster? The apparent return of Brazil to an overtly pro-United States foreign policy attitude and the conciliatory US vote in favour of the Argentine UN resolution on the Malvinas in the closing weeks of 1982, accompanied by talk of US support for Brazil's application to the IMF for a $6.7 billion loan and the possible resumption of US military activities in Brazil all implied a tightening up of US relations with Latin America which President Reagan's December visit to the sub-continent was plainly intended to endorse.[41] A similar linking of emergency financial assistance to political concessions is also becoming evident in US relations with Mexico, and suggests interesting questions to be asked about the politics of recent Mexican tariff reductions.[42] The dismal GATT talks also revived talk of a possible Pacific Basin preferential zone, in which Australia, New Zealand, Japan, ASEAN, and some of the West Coast Latin American republics might attempt to generate the rapid growth and integration which had eluded the wider international community.[43]

Such signs of a return to bilateralism and the United States nightmare of rival blocs are, of course, to be observed at every turn in the post-war world, and have often been built up into plausible neo-Leninist analyses of a new imperialism.[44] They have just as often been confounded by the durability and extent of the US commitment in Europe, both military and economic, and only time, elections, and the final outcome of East–West arms talks will tell whether this conjuncture is any different from its predecessors.

Third-World Indebtedness and the IMF

If the USA does ultimately abandon its post-1945 multilateralism in favour of a more restricted hemispheric role, one important reason may prove to have been its final loss of control over the international institutions which it originally created to police the international economy. The North Americans have had great difficulties in recent years in holding their own in trade negotiations within the GATT against the increasingly well concerted and prevailingly statist views of the EEC. In the IMF, too, the United States appears to be losing its grip and to be taking it badly, and this at a time when the Fund has become far more important as regulator of the world economy and lender of the last resort to LDCs than it was in the mid-1970s.

The Group of 77 have continued to press for much the same package of reforms as ever: increased IMF quotas, more SDRs more equitably distributed, a further shift away from project aid by the World Bank, and an easing of IMF policy conditions. But it has not been Group of 77 or UNCTAD pressure which has changed the function and policy of the IMF. Indeed UNCTAD efforts to engage in debate on monetary matters have been pointedly ignored by the DCs.[45] Rather, the forces for change have been the crisis in private bank dealings with the non-oil LDCs and the lending power of Saudi Arabia.

The second round of oil price increases in 1978 and 1979 and the highly restrictive monetary policies with which the USA and other DCs responded set up severe strains in the world banking system. Instead of the recovery on which they had counted to enable the major Latin American debtors to service their loans, private bankers encountered a new climate of high real interest rates. As the end of the decade approached, the position was further aggravated as OPEC surpluses began to dry up because of an oil glut brought about by the continuing world recession.

By 1978 it had already become common practice for the formerly incautious international bankers to make loans to third-world states conditional on their first being granted IMF credits and accepting the policy conditions laid down by Fund officials. In short, third-world states which had once avoided IMF conditionality by resort to private money markets had now to accept it as entrance fee. This might seem to have been a victory for the United States government, which had traditionally worked closely with the IMF and the World Bank to discipline the impecunious and instil sound liberal economic principles. Traditional grumblings about the imperialist role of the Fund as a United States proxy have continued to be heard, yet there are signs that this stereotype of the Left no longer accurately captures the IMF of the 1980s.

The story begins with Arab attempts, common enough at the time in many international organizations, to secure observer status for the PLO at meetings of the IMF and the World Bank. First launched in 1979, this campaign gathered support over the next year and led to a major skirmish with the USA during the weeks leading up to the annual Fund and Bank meetings in September 1980.[46] What made the PLO question of especial importance in the IMF was the fact that the surpluses of Saudi Arabia and a dwindling handful of low-absorptive OPEC states had for several years been channelled through the IMF to help solve the balance of payments problems of the non-oil LDCs. The Saudis therefore possessed in this forum, as in no other, a weighty sanction. Early in September, Saudi Arabia, Kuwait, and two other OPEC members duly announced to the IMF directors that they would make no further loans to the Fund because of its failure to grant observer status to the PLO.[47]

The trap into which the USA had fallen began to become clear. If the administration were to give way on the PLO question in order to remove the OPEC cash embargo, Congress would almost certainly vote down proposals currently before it designed to enable President Carter to increase the US IMF quota and contribute to the IDA replenishment. But if, as was just possible, the quota increase were to go through without US participation, then the IMF votes controlled by the Americans, currently about 20 per cent, would fall still further, to about 12 per cent, while Group of 77 votes would rise to 45 per cent of the total.[48] If, on the other hand, the Carter administration were to stand firm against the Arabs it might very well have to acquiesce in some later side payments to persuade them to drop the embargo. This would almost certainly involve a permanent increase in Saudi power within the IMF, which the US had been at pains to resist in the past.

In the event, the PLO was excluded at the end of September 1980. But by the turn of the year it was evident that the IMF was running short of funds, and a further meeting to discuss the PLO issue in January 1981, although giving no public indication of any resolution of the deadlock, was immediately followed by a resumption of talks on a Saudi credit for the Fund, to be coupled with an increase in the Saudi share of IMF votes from 1.75 to 3.5 per cent, giving the right to a permanent seat on the executive board.[49]

This tactical defeat for the USA was rapidly followed by another, as Group of 77 states combined with minor DCs to defeat Sir Geoffrey Howe, the favoured United States candidate for the chairmanship of the key policy-making interim committee of the IMF, electing instead the Canadian finance minister, Allan MacEachen, who had earned a favourable reputation in the Third World by his joint-chairmanship of the CIEC in 1976 and 1977.[50] Still further evidence of the incipient marginalization of the USA came at the 1981 annual meeting, where a broadside from the new Reagan administration attacking the recent speeding up of Fund loans to the Third World on perceptibly easier terms was shrugged off by the interim committee.[51] Finally, the US administration, 'hard-nosed to the point of self-delusion' was nevertheless unable to hold the 1982 increase in quotas to 20 per cent as it had hoped, and was indeed brought to some appreciation of the extent of the world financial crisis and the size of the gap to be filled by IMF funds as Mexico, followed by several other major debtors, came to the brink of default on its external debts in the closing months of 1982.[52]

Whether the virtual doubling of IMF resources hastily agreed early in 1983 will prevent a major bank crisis in the West remains to be seen.[53] But it does show that the naïvely neo-liberal Reagan administration can no longer dictate the policy of the IMF, and suggests that even a more moderate US government might encounter serious problems in again bending this once captive international organization to its will.

Conclusion

How one evaluates the utility of the North–South dialogue, from whatever standpoint, depends upon what the central objectives of the participants are considered to have been: whether economic or political; short- or long-term.

A number of ingenious papers in the economics journals have advanced neo-liberal arguments showing that if the Group of 77 were ever to achieve their stated objectives in the UNCTAD IPC and elsewhere the effect would be to diminish income in a majority of its members, advantaging only small groups of relatively wealthy LDCs.[54] From the same direction come familiar arguments about growth and distribution. Economic growth provides additional resources with which to solve the essentially distributive problems of political life, it is urged. To place equity ahead of growth is to restrict the range of political solutions needlessly in the long term. So runs the basic argument; and it is directed against the whole range of southern demands for regulation of commodity markets, seabed exploration and mining, and direct foreign investment, all of which are thought likely to inhibit investment to the ultimate cost of both North and South. A rather different line of attack, sometimes found in conjunction with those mentioned already, accuses the Group of 77 and its call for an NIEO of irrelevance rather than diseconomy, suggesting that political changes within individual southern states are far more likely to bring about economic development than any reforms or extensions of international law.[55]

It is possible to dodge or parry these charges to a point. To show that NIEO demands make little economic sense is not to demonstrate the ignorance or irrationality of their advocates. It leaves open the possibility that the NIEO proposals may have been no more than aggressive negotiating stances to be promptly abandoned in favour of advantageous compromise positions. But this is not altogether convincing. Extreme initial negotiating positions are only likely to elicit concessions if they are believed to be genuine by the other side, and many Group of 77 demands either lacked this credibility from the start or soon lost it in skirmishes with western economists. Moreover, the substantial rate of concession required to move from extreme initial positions to more moderate ones may signal weakness to an opponent, reducing his willingness to compromise without still further concessions. Whichever way one looks at it, the charismatic advantages of an audacious platform were likely to be far outweighed by its technical weaknesses once the stage of detailed negotiations was reached.

The argument about growth may also be side-stepped after a fashion by pointing to the more illiberal aspects of DC policies. Why should third-world proposals for regulating a marginal fraction of world trade and investment be blamed for global stagnation when the quantitative impact of DC monetarism and protectionism must far outweigh their slight effects? But two wrongs do not make a right, and it is probably true that a general liberalization of international trade, though politically improbable, would indeed produce more rapid economic growth for a time at least.

As for the charge of irrelevance, it may be answered with the standard Latin American *dependencia* argument that, while domestic government policy in each state may be the crucial current determinant of economic development, it is the long history of its relations with the world economy that has shaped the productive and class structure of each state and so constrained the range of possible policies. Yet neither of these opposed positions has much need of international organization or international law to explain the evolution of dependency in the Third World, except as a subordinate instrument of Yankee imperialism.

One way out of the dilemma posed by the poor showing of the NIEO proposals as potential economic policy is to view the whole North–South dialogue, since 1973 at least, as a threat against the North more than a programme for the South. By putting their weight behind a half-baked set of UNCTAD proposals the Arab states in OPEC could achieve a double advantage. Because of their ideological differences over the efficacy of economic planning the same set of proposals would appear attractive to third-world states whose diplomatic support was needed against Israel while at the same time being perceived as a threat—and a serious threat—by Israel's powerful ally, the USA. It did not matter that the proposals were half-baked, since they were only to be taken up for short-term political advantage; indeed it helped, because it upset the rational Americans all the more.

But while it surely contains some element of truth, a cynical scenario such as this, in which the great majority of the Group of 77 are pawns to the Arab oil states or, perhaps, to the NICs, as these more powerful LDCs pursue their particular diplomatic objectives, is not the whole truth. Governments of the weaker third-world states are neither so poorly informed that they will naïvely subscribe to NIEO proposals that would ultimately inhibit their own economic development nor so feeble that they will act as unpaid lobby fodder for Saudi Arabia or Brazil at the United Nations.

There is a third possibility, and this is that the Dialogue has been in essence a struggle about sovereignty in which the central concern of the South has been to gain control of international organizations and international law originally created by the leading DCs to order their mutual transactions, and to direct it instead towards affirmation of the sanctity, autonomy, and indivisibility of the nation state. This view is attractive to fabians who (though they may not share third-world nationalist aspirations) are able to imagine a slow process of change in which a preamble here and a clause there gradually mount up, in spite of apparent southern defeats, until we find ourselves in a world where a host of small but irreversible modifications in the regimes governing trade, investment, nuclear proliferation and the rest have together bound the Gulliver of the North hand and foot.

If the main southern objective has been a stealthy revolution against the post-imperial vestiges of liberal cosmopolitanism, then the paradox of their dis-economic proposals in UNCTAD and elsewhere is resolved and the universal southern support for the Group of 77 accounted for. Sovereignty is to be affirmed even at some economic cost. It is independence, rather than economic growth, which is believed to provide increased freedom of action for governments wrestling with the problem of distribution. And this nationalist ideology, with clear origins in the anti-colonial struggle, is persuasive throughout the Third World.

Yet there remains the question of tactics. The southern assault in international forums has been much noisier than it need have been. The South has displayed considerable skill in maintaining the voting unity of the Group of 77, in running single issues in multiple forums, in widening agendas and extending the scope of the Dialogue to embrace functional areas as far apart as opiates and nuclear non-proliferation; but it has also damaged the slow but steady progress of its programme on numerous occasions, insisting on fully ratified treaties when guidelines or informal codes of conduct would have gained more adherents and had much the same long-term impact on national law-making, and, more damaging still, laying constant stress on its own weakness.

This, like so much of the Group of 77 style, was an inheritance from the strategy of the Latin American republics in the 1950s, which had emphasized their own powerlessness and the small effort it would cost the USA to improve matters. It was ineffective because, as John Powelson has pointed out,

> North Americans—particularly those of the generation now in political power—have been taught to admire strength and to despise weakness . . . [indeed] the legitimate destruction of the weak has become sanctified in political and economic theory.[56]

But by the time this somewhat hysterical pose was dropped it had served to alienate élites in the United States and elsewhere to the point where they would see their own interests damaged before they made real concessions to the South. For the stiff reluctance of the Americans to co-operate and compromise in the creation of international agreements is hard to explain in purely material terms, since any financial losses stemming from substantial concessions to the South would in all probability be more than compensated for by the fresh opportunities to co-opt and control southern states which a more relaxed and open-handed policy would bring. A tactical error by the South, therefore, coinciding with a period of American insecurity and self-doubt, introduced what now seems an ineradicable element of psychological conflict into which might otherwise have been a relatively smooth transition to a much looser though still US-dominated western system.

Excessively noisy rhetoric coupled with undue emphasis on southern weakness may be seen to have compromised the negotiating position of the Group of 77. On balance, the harm they have done to the third-world cause by alienating western governing élites probably far outweighs any support they may have generated among the rank and file of western legislators, trade unionists and intellectuals, most of whom have turned their attention to other issues since the 1970s. So the Dialogue continues haltingly. As a means to third-world economic development it ranks well below structural reform in the South and liberalization of northern trading regimes in its potential. As a political instrument for the aggrandizement of leading states in the Third World and the resolution of regional conflicts, it has proved indecisive. It remains to be seen whether it will result in a permanent shift towards statism in the emphasis of international law and a greater voice in international organizations for the South, but it seems unlikely that the northern acquiescence needed if such a change is to take place will be secured unless the United States is able to resolve a long agenda of problems concerning East–West relations, relations with its NATO allies and OECD trading partners, and the condition of its domestic economy. In the beginning it was northern weakness and vulnerability which allowed the South a foothold and set the Dialogue in motion. Ironically, it may turn out that the failure of the DCs to solve their problems will reduce their capacity to make concessions by weakening their economies and invalidating the network of international co-operation which has been a chief objective of the southern campaign.

Notes

1. *Financial Times*, 19, 29 October 1982.
2. *Financial Times*, 3 January 1980; *Guardian*, 21 October 1982.
3. Ursula Wassermann, 'WIPO: the Exclusion of South Africa?', *Journal of World Trade Law*, 14 (1980) 78–80; *Financial Times*, 10 March 1981.
4. *Guardian*, 22 October 1979.
5. *Financial Times*, 28 October 1980.
6. *Financial Times*, 24 September 1981.
7. *Guardian*, 9 February 1982.
8. Wassermann, op. cit.
9. *Financial Times*, 26 March, 16 April 1981.
10. *Financial Times*, 14 December 1982.
11. *Financial Times*, 25 August 1982.
12. *Financial Times*, 27 October 1982.

13. *Financial Times*, 25 and 26 August and 1 September 1982.
14. Christopher Hayman, 'International Shipping', in R. P. Barston and Patricia Birnie, eds, *The Maritime Dimension* (London, Allen & Unwin, 1980), p. 135; Stephen C. Neff, 'The UN Code of Conduct for Liner Conferences', *Journal of World Trade Law*, 14 (1980), p. 403.
15. *Guardian*, 20 April 1982.
16. *Financial Times*, 4 May and 12 November 1982; *Guardian*, 27 May 1981.
17. *Guardian*, 21 August 1979; *Financial Times*, 23 August 1979.
18. A. F. Ewing, 'UNIDO III', *Journal of World Trade Law*, 14 (1980), 251–4; *Guardian*, 21 January 1980.
19. Wassermann, 'WIPO: the Exclusion of South Africa?'; Ursula Wassermann, 'WIPO: Diplomatic Patent Conference', *Journal of World Trade Law*, 14 (1980), 254–6.
20. Anon., 'WIPO: revision of the Paris Convention', *Journal of World Trade Law*, 16 (1982), 180–2.
21. For further details see Dennis Thompson, 'The UNCTAD Code on Transfer of Technology', *Journal of World Trade Law*, 16 (1982), 311–37.
22. Ronald S. Katz, 'Financial Arrangements for Seabed Mining Companies: an NIEO study', *Journal of World Trade Law*, 13 (1979), 209–22.
23. *Financial Times*, 4 May 1979.
24. Per Magnus Wijkman, 'UNCLOS and the Redistribution of Ocean Wealth', *Journal of World Trade Law*, 16 (1982), 27–48.
25. *Financial Times*, 30 January 1982.
26. *Financial Times*, 9 March 1982.
27. *Financial Times*, 21 October 1982.
28. Ursula Wassermann, 'Law of the Sea Convention Adopted', *Journal of World Trade Law*, 16 (1982), 440–4.
29. *Guardian*, 30 November 1978; *Financial Times*, 12 March 1979.
30. *Financial Times*, 17 October 1979.
31. *Financial Times*, 17 and 19 October 1979 and 15 January 1980. Some feeling for the complexity of the issues involved and the strength of the US defence may be gained from Sue Cameron's excellent reporting in the *Financial Times*, especially for 25 September 1979.
32. *Financial Times*, 8 and 10 April and 29 May 1981.
33. *Guardian*, 19 November 1981. A surge mechanism would inhibit, if not deter, attempts by textiles firms based in Hong Kong, for example, to utilize the quotas of minor exporters by DFI.
34. Anon., 'GATT: Third Multifibre Arrangement', *Journal of World Trade Law*, 16 (1982), 178–80.
35. *Financial Times*, 5 August 1982.
36. *Financial Times*, 24 November 1982.
37. *Financial Times*, 2 December 1982.
38. *Financial Times*, 17 January 1983.
39. *Financial Times*, 17 September 1982.
40. *Financial Times*, 30 November 1982.
41. *Guardian*, 4 November and 1 and 3 December; *Financial Times*, 16 November and 1 December 1982.
42. *Financial Times*, 5 November 1982, 19 January 1983.
43. *Financial Times*, 27 November 1982.
44. See, for example, Mary Kaldor, *The Disintegrating West* (Harmondsworth, Penguin, 1978).

45. *Guardian*, 11 August 1980.
46. *Financial Times*, 5, 16, and 22 September 1980; *Guardian*, 6 and 10 September 1980.
47. *Guardian*, 6 September 1980.
48. *Financial Times*, 16 September 1980.
49. *Financial Times*, 21 January, 7 February, and 31 March 1981; *Guardian*, 4 February 1981.
50. *Financial Times*, 27 May 1981.
51. *Financial Times*, 28 September 1981.
52. *Financial Times*, 28 September 1981, 26 November 1982.
53. *Financial Times*, 30 November 1982, 19 January 1983; *Guardian*, 11 January 1983.
54. For a general exposition of this view see Sidney Weintraub, 'The New International Economic Order: the Beneficiaries', *World Development*, 7 (1979), 247–58. On the Law of the Sea, see Per Magnus Wijkman, 'UNCLOS and the Redistribution of Ocean Wealth', *Journal of World Trade Law*, 16 (1982), 27–48.
55. This view is to be found on the Left as well as the Right, though it is far from universally held at either extreme of the political spectrum. See Harry Magdoff, 'Limits of International Reform', *Monthly Review*, 30 (1978), 1–11, and Sidney Weintraub, 'What Life is Left in the North–South Dialogue?', *The World Economy*, 2 (1980), 453–65.
56. John P. Powelson, 'The International Politics of Latin American Economics', in L. E. Di Marco, ed., *International Economics and Development: Essays in Honor of Raúl Prebisch* (New York and London, Academic Press, 1972), pp. 430, 431. John White, 'The New International Economic Order: What Is It?', *International Affairs*, 54 (1978), p. 630, notes the same 'deep-seated and wrong belief in the ineluctable superiority of the developed countries' negotiating hand'. A most evocative and thought-provoking treatment of the same theme occurs in Rebecca West's *Black Lamb and Grey Falcon: the Record of a Journey through Yugoslavia in 1937* (London, Macmillan, 1942), II, p. 295, *et seq.*

BIBLIOGRAPHY

Abbot, George, C., 'Recent Developments in the International Monetary System and Their Implications for International Economic Relations', *Journal of Economic Studies*, **6** (1979), 129–54.

Agmon, T. and C. P. Kindleberger, eds, *Multinationals from Small Countries* (Cambridge, Mass., MIT, 1977).

Ajami, Fouad, 'The Fate of Non-Alignment', *Foreign Affairs*, **59** (1980/1), 366–85.

Amuzegar, Johangir, 'A Requiem for the North–South Conference', *Foreign Affairs*, **56** (1977), 136–59.

Anell, Lars and Birgitta Nygren, *The Developing Countries and the World Economic Order* (London, Frances Pinter, 1980).

Anon., 'South–South Dialogue: a brief report', *Third World Quarterly*, **1** (1979), 117–22.

Anon., 'GATT: Third Multifibre Arrangement', *Journal of World Trade Law*, **16** (1982), 178–80.

Anon., 'WIPO: Revision of the Paris Convention', *Journal of World Trade Law*, **16** (1982), 180–2.

Ansari, Javed, 'Environmental Characteristics and Organization Ideology: UNCTAD and the lessons of 1964', *British Journal of International Studies*, **4** (1978), 135–60.

Arndt, H. W., 'Economic Development: a Semantic History', *Economic Development and Cultural Change*, **29** (1981), 457–66.

Asher, Robert E., Walter M. Kotschnig, William Adams Brown, Jr, *et al.*, *The United Nations and Economic and Social Cooperation* (Washington DC, The Brookings Institution, 1957).

Aufricht, Hans, *The International Monetary Fund: Legal Bases, Structure, Functions* (London, Stevens & Sons, 1964).

Bailey, Sydney D., 'The UN Security Council: evolving practice', *The World Today*, **34** (1978), 100–6.

Bairoch, Paul, *The Economic Development of the Third World since 1900* (London, Methuen, 1975).

Balasubramanyam, V. N., 'Transfer of Technology: the UNCTAD Arguments in Perspective', *The World Economy*, **1** (1977), 69–80.

Barston, R. P., 'The Law of the Sea Conference: the Search for New Regimes', in R. P. Barston and P. Birnie, eds, *The Maritime Dimension* (London, Allen & Unwin, 1980), pp. 154–68.

Bauer, P. T., *Dissent on Development* (Student edition, London, Weidenfeld & Nicolson, 1976).

Bird, Graham, 'Financial Flows to Developing Countries: the Role of the International Monetary Fund', *Review of International Studies*, **7** (1981).

Birnie, P. W., 'The Law of the Sea Before and After UNCLOS I and UNCLOS II', in R. P. Barston and P. Birnie, eds, *The Maritime Dimension* (London, Allen & Unwin, 1980), pp. 8–26.

Bloch, Henry Simon, 'Regional Development Financing', *International Organization*, **22** (1968), 182–203, reprinted in Richard N. Gardner and M. F. Millikan, eds, *The Global Partnership: International Agencies and Economic Development* (New York, Praeger, 1968).

Blough, Roy, 'The World Bank Group', *International Organization*, 22 (1968), 152–81.

Bronfenbrenner, M., 'Review Article: Predatory Poverty on the Offensive—the UNCTAD Record', *Economic Development and Cultural Change*, 24 (1976), 825–31.

Brown, C., *The Political and Social Economy of Commodity Control* (London, Macmillan, 1980).

Calleo, David P. and Benjamin M. Rowland, *America and the World Political Economy: Atlantic Dreams and National Realities* (Bloomington, Ind., and London, Indiana University Press, 1973).

Cameron, Duncan, 'The Reform of International Money', *International Journal*, 34 (1978–9), 90–109.

Cameron, Duncan, 'Special Drawing Rights', *International Journal*, 36 (1981), 713–31.

Carré, Olivier, 'Steps towards Peace', (1982) in Maxime Rodinson, *Israel and the Arabs* (Harmondsworth, Penguin, 1972; reprinted with additional material, 1982).

Chomsky, Noam, *et al.*, *Superpowers in Collision: the New Cold War* (Harmondsworth, Penguin, 1982).

Cutajar, Michael Zammit and Alison Franks, *The Less Developed Countries in World Trade* (London, ODI Ltd, 1967).

Cleveland, Harold van B. and Wilt B. Brittain, 'Are the LDCs in over their Heads?', *Foreign Affairs*, 55 (1977), 732–50.

Curry, Robert L., Jr, 'Africa's External Debt Situation', *Journal of Modern African Studies*, 17 (1979), 15–28.

Davey, Brian, *The Economic Development of India* (London, Spokesman Books, 1975).

Díaz-Alejandro, Carlos, 'The Post-1971 International Financial System and the Less Developed Countries', in G. K. Helleiner, ed., *A World Divided: the Less Developed Countries in the International Economy* (Cambridge, Cambridge University Press, 1976).

Di Marco, Luis Eugenio, 'The Evolution of Prebisch's Economic Thought', in L. E. Di Marco, ed., *International Economics and Development: Essays in Honor of Raúl Prebisch* (New York and London, Academic Press, 1972), pp. 3–13.

Economic Commission for Latin America, *The Economic Development of Latin America and its Principal Problems* (Lake Success, NY, United Nations Department of Economic Affairs, 1950).

Evans, Peter, *Dependent Development: the alliance of multinational, state, and local capital in Brazil* (Princeton, NJ, Princeton University Press, 1979).

Ewing, A. F., 'UNIDO III', *Journal of World Trade Law*, 14 (1980), 251–4.

Farrands, Chris, 'The Political Economy of the Multifibre Arrangement', in Christopher Stevens, ed., *EEC and the Third World: a Survey—II. Hunger in the World* (London, Hodder & Stoughton, 1982), pp. 87–101.

Feld, Werner J., *Multinational Corporations and UN Politics: the Quest for Codes of Conduct* (New York, Pergamon, 1980).

Finger, J. M. and Dean A. Derosa, 'The Compensatory Finance Facility and Export Instability', *Journal of World Trade Law*, 14 (1980), 14–22.

Fishlow, Albert, 'A New International Economic Order: What Kind?', in Albert Fishlow, *et al.*, *Rich and Poor Nations in the World Economy* (New York, McGraw-Hill, 1978).

Flanders, M. June, 'Prebisch on Protectionism: an Evaluation', *Economic Journal*, 74 (1964), 305–26.

Frank, Charles R., Jr, and Mary Baird, 'Foreign Aid: Its Speckled Past and Future Prospects', *International Organization*, 29 (1975), 133–67.

Frank, Isaiah, 'The "Graduation" Issue for LDCs', *Journal of World Trade Law*, 13 (1979), 289–302.

Friedeberg, A. S., *The United Nations Conference on Trade and Development of 1964* (Rotterdam, Rotterdam University Press, 1969).

Frieden, Jeff, 'Third World Indebted Industrialization: International Finance and State Capitalism in Mexico, Brazil, Algeria, and South Korea', *International Organization*, 35 (1981), 407–31.

Furtado, Celso, *Economic Development of Latin America: a Survey from Colonial Times to the Cuban Revolution* (Cambridge, Cambridge University Press, 1970).

Gardner, Richard N., 'The United Nations Conference on Trade and Development', *International Organization*, 22 (1968), 99–130, reprinted in Gardner, Richard N. and Millikan, M. F., eds, *The Global Partnership: International Agencies and Economic Development* (New York, Praeger, 1968).

Gavshon, Arthur, *Crisis in Africa: Battleground of East and West* (Harmondsworth, Penguin, 1981).

Goodwin, Geoffrey, 'The UNCTAD Common Fund—Challenge and Response', *The World Today* (November, 1977), 425–32.

Graham, Anila, 'The Transfer of Technology: Test Case in North–South Dialogue: a Historical Review', *Journal of International Affairs*, 33 (1979), 1–17.

Grogan, F. O., *International Trade in Temperate Zone Products* (Edinburgh, Oliver & Boyd, 1972).

Halliday, Fred, *Iran: Dictatorship and Development* (Harmondsworth, Penguin, 1979).

Hallwood, Paul and Stuart Sinclair, *Oil, Debt, and Development: OPEC in the Third World* (London, Allen & Unwin, 1981).

Hayman, Christopher, 'International Shipping', in R. P. Barston and Patricia Birnie, eds, *The Maritime Dimension* (London, Allen & Unwin, 1980), pp. 128–41.

Hayter, Teresa, *Aid as Imperialism* (Harmondsworth, Penguin, 1971).

Hayter, Teresa, *The Creation of World Poverty: an alternative view to the Brandt Report* (London, Pluto Press, 1981).

Henderson, P. D., 'Survival, Development and the Report of the Brandt Commission', *The World Economy*, 3 (1980), 87–117.

Hewitt, Adrian and Christopher Stevens, 'The Second Lomé Convention', in Christopher Stevens, ed., *EEC and the Third World: a Survey*, I (London, Hodder & Stoughton, 1981), pp. 30–59.

Hilton, Stanley E., *Brazil and the Great Powers, 1930–1939: the Politics of Trade Rivalry* (Austin, Tex. and London, University of Texas Press, 1975).

Hope, Ronald, 'The Political Economy of Marine Transportation', in Douglas M. Johnston, ed., *Marine Policy and the Coastal Community: the impact of the Law of the Sea* (London, Croom Helm, 1976), pp. 103–43.

Hutchings, Raymond, 'Soviet Arms Exports to the Third World: a pattern and its implications', *The World Today*, 34 (October 1978), 378–89.

Independent Commission on International Development Issues (Chairman, Willy Brandt), *North–South: a Programme for Survival* (London, Pan, 1980).

International Bank for Reconstruction and Development, *World Development Report, 1981* (New York, IBRD, 1981).

Isaacs, Asher, *International Trade: Tariffs and Commercial Policies* (Chicago, Richard D. Irwin, 1948), pp. 269–73.

Jalée, Pierre, *The Pillage of the Third World* (Paris, 1965; English translation by Mary Klopper, New York and London, Monthly Review Press, 1968).

Joekes, S. and C. H. Kirkpatrick, 'The Results of UNCTAD V', *Journal of World Trade Law*, 13 (1979), 535–49.

Jones, C. A., ' "Business Imperialism" and Argentina, 1875–1900: a Theoretical Note', *Journal of Latin American Studies*, 12 (1980), 437–44.

Kaiser, David E., *Economic Diplomacy and the Origins of the Second World War: Germany, Britain, France and Eastern Europe, 1930–1939* (Princeton, NJ, Princeton University Press, 1980).

Kaldor, Mary, *The Disintegrating West* (Harmondsworth, Penguin, 1978).

Kapoor, M. C. and Rajan Saxena, 'Taming the Multinationals in India', *Journal of World Trade Law*, 13 (1979), 170–8.

Katz, Ronald S., 'Financial Arrangements for Seabed Mining Companies: an NIEO Study', *Journal of World Trade Law*, 13 (1979), 209–22.

Killick, Tony, 'Eurocurrency Market Recycling of OPEC Surpluses to Developing Countries: Fact or Myth?', in C. Stevens, ed., *EEC and the Third World* (London, Hodder & Stoughton, 1981), pp. 92–104.

Krishnamurti, R., 'UNCTAD as a Negotiating Institution', *Journal of World Trade Law*, 15 (1981), 3–40.

Kumar, Krishna and Maxwell G. McLoed, eds, *Multinationals from Developing Countries* (Lexington, Mass., Lexington Books, 1981).

Laszlo, Ervin, Robert Baker Jr, Elliott Eisenberg and Venkata Raman, *The Objectives of the New International Economic Order* (New York, Pergamon, 1978, for UNITAR).

Leifer, Michael, 'The Paradox of ASEAN: a security organization without the structure of an alliance', *The Round Table*, 271 (1978), 261–8.

Levitt, Kari, *The Silent Surrender: the Multinational Corporation in Canada* (Toronto, Liveright Publishing Corp., 1970).

Lewis, W. A., *Aspects of Industrialization* (Cairo, National Bank of Egypt, 1953).

Little, I. M. D., 'Distributive Justice and the New International Economic Order', in Peter Oppenheimer, ed., *Issues in International Economics* (London, Routledge & Kegan Paul, 1978), pp. 37–53.

Little, I., Tibor Scitovsky and Maurice Scott, *Industry and Trade in Some Developing Countries: a comparative study* (Oxford, Oxford University Press, 1970).

McNicol, David L., *Commodity Agreements and Price Stabilization* (Lexington, Mass., Lexington Books, 1978).

MacPhee, Craig R., 'Martin Bronfenbrenner on UNCTAD and the GSP: comment', and M. Bronfenbrenner, 'Rejoinder to Prof. MacPhee', *Economic Development and Cultural Change*, 27 (1979), 357–63, 365–6.

Magdoff, Harry, 'Limits of International Reform', *Monthly Review*, 30 (1978), 1–11.

Meier, Gerald M., 'The "Jamaica Agreement", International Monetary Reform, and the Developing Countries', *Journal of International Law and Economics*, 11 (1977), 67–89.

Mendelsohn, M. Stefan, *Money on the Move: the Modern International Capital Market* (New York, McGraw-Hill, 1980).

Miles, Edward, 'The Dynamics of Global Ocean Politics', in Douglas M. Johnston, ed., *Marine Policy and the Coastal Community: the Impact of the Law of the Sea* (London, Croom Helm, 1976), pp. 147–81.

Moss, Alfred, G. and H. N. M. Winston, eds, *A New International Economic Order: selected documents, 1954–1975* (New York, UNITAR, 1976).

Nair, V. M., 'Havana Summit Shows up Non-Aligned Divisions', *The Round Table*, 277 (1980), 99–101.

Nappi, Carmine, *Commodity Market Controls: a Historical Review* (Lexington, Mass., Lexington Books, 1979).

Neff, Stephen C., 'The UN Code of Conduct for Liner Conferences', *Journal of World Trade Law*, 14 (1980), 398–423.

Negandhi, Anant R., *Quest for Survival and Growth: a Comparative Study of American, European, and Japanese Multinationals* (New York, Praeger, 1979).

Nye, Joseph S., 'UNCTAD: Poor Nations' Pressure Group', in Cox and Jacobson, *et al.*, *The Anatomy of Influence*, pp. 334–70.

Paine, Tom, *Rights of Man* (Harmondsworth, Penguin, 1969), p. 26.

Payer, Cheryl, *The Debt Trap: the IMF and the Third World* (Harmondsworth, Penguin, 1974).

Petras, James F. and Morris H. Morely, 'The Rise and Fall of Regional Economic Nationalism in the Andean Countries, 1969–1977', *Social and Economic Studies*, 27 (1978), 153–67.

Platt, D. C. M., ed., *Business Imperialism, 1840–1930: an Inquiry Based on British Experience in Latin America* (Oxford, Oxford University Press, 1977), pp. 119–55.

Powelson, John P., 'The International Politics of Latin American Economics', in L. E. Di Marco, ed., *International Economics and Development: Essays in Honor of Raúl Prebisch* (New York and London, Academic Press, 1972).

Powelson, John P., 'The Strange Persistence of the "Terms of Trade" ', *Inter-American Economic Affairs*, 30 (1977), 17–28.

Powers, Richard J., 'United Nations Voting Alignments: a New Equilibrium', *Western Political Quarterly*, 33 (1980), 167–84.

Prebisch, Raúl, 'Commercial Policy in the Underdeveloped Countries', *American Economic Review*, 44 (1959), 251–73.

Prebisch, Raúl, *Towards a New Trade Policy for Latin America* (New York, United Nations, 1964).

Price, Victoria Curzon, 'Surplus Capacity and What the Tokyo Round Failed to Settle', *The World Economy*, 2 (1979), 305–18.

Ramphal, Shridath S., 'Not by Unity Alone: the Case for Third World Organization', *Third World Quarterly*, 1 (1979), 43–52.

Ravenhill, John, 'Asymmetrical Interdependence: Renegotiating the Lomé Convention', *International Journal*, 35 (1979/80), 150–69.

Root, Franklin R., *International Trade and Investment*, 4th edn (Cincinnati, Ohio, South-Western Publishing Co., 1978).

Rothstein, Robert L., *Global Bargaining: UNCTAD and the Quest for a New International Economic Order* (Princeton, NJ, Princeton University Press, 1979).

Rowe, J. W. F., *Primary Commodities in International Trade* (Cambridge, Cambridge University Press, 1965).

Rubin, Barry, *Paved with Good Intentions: the American experience and Iran* (Harmondsworth, Penguin, 1980).

Sauvant, Karl P., *Changing Priorities on the International Agenda: the New International Economic Order* (New York, Pergamon, 1981).

Sauvant, Karl P. and Hajo Hasenplug, eds, *The New International Economic Order: Confrontation or Cooperation between North and South?* (Boulder, Col., Westview, 1977).

Servan-Schreiber, Jean-Jacques, *The American Challenge* (Harmondsworth, Penguin, 1970 (first published 1968)).

Seymour, Ian, *OPEC: Instrument of Change* (London, Macmillan, 1980).

Sharan, Vyuptakesh, 'Multinational Corporations and the Balance of Payments Problem in a Developing Host Country: an Indian Experience', *Indian Economic Journal*, 26 (1978), 199-215.

Shihata, I. and Robert Mabro, 'The OPEC Aid Record', *World Development*, 7 (1979), 161-73.

Simmons, Luiz R. S. and Abdul A. Said, eds, *Drugs, Politics and Diplomacy: the International Connection* (Beverley Hills and London, Sage, 1974).

Singer, H. W., 'The Common Fund Debate', *The Round Table*, 271 (1978), 229-35.

Singer, Hans and Javed Ansari, *Rich and Poor Countries* (London, George Allen & Unwin, 1977).

Smart, Ian, 'Janus: the Nuclear God', *The World Today*, 3 (1978), 118-27.

Smith, G. W. and G. R. Schink, 'The International Tin Agreement: a Reassessment', *Economic Journal*, 86 (1976), 715-28.

Smith, Ian, 'Sugar Markets in Disarray', *Journal of World Trade Law*, 9 (1975), 41-62.

Smyth, Douglas C., 'The Global Economy and the Third World—Coalition or Cleavage?', *World Politics*, 29 (1977), 584-603.

Solberg, Carl, 'Tariff and Politics in Argentina, 1916-1930', *Hispanic-American Historical Review*, 53 (1973), 260-84.

Spero, Joan E., *The Politics of International Economic Relations* (London, Allen & Unwin, 1978).

Stewart, Frances and Arjun Sengupta, *International Financial Cooperation: a framework for change* (London and Boulder, Col., Frances Pinter, 1982).

Stockholm International Peace Research Institute, *The Arms Trade with the Third World* (Harmondsworth, Penguin, 1975).

Stortz, Pat, 'The Association of South-East Asian Nations: its Development, Achievements, and Prospects' (unpublished MA dissertation, University of Warwick, 1979).

Strange, Susan, 'IMF: Monetary Managers', in Robert W. Cox and Harold K. Jacobson, *et al.*, *The Anatomy of Influence: Decision-Making in International Organization* (New Haven and London, Yale University Press, 1973), pp. 263-97.

Strange, Susan, 'Who Runs World Shipping?', *International Affairs*, 52 (1976), 346-67.

Streeten, Paul, 'World Trade in Agricultural Commodities and the Terms of Trade with Industrial Goods' in Nurul Islam, ed., *Agricultural Policy in Developing Countries* (London, Wiley, 1974).

Streeten, Paul, 'The Dynamics of the New Poor Power', in G. K. Helleiner, *A World Divided: the Less Developed Countries in the International Economy* (Cambridge, Cambridge University Press, 1976), pp. 77-88.

Thompson, Dennis, 'The UNCTAD Code on Transfer of Technology', *Journal of World Trade Law*, 16 (1982), 311-37.

Turner, Louis, 'The North–South Dialogue', *The World Today*, **32** (February 1976), 81–3.

Turner, Louis, 'Oil and the North–South Dialogue', *The World Today*, **33** (February 1977), 52–61.

Turner, Louis and Audrey Parry, 'The Next Steps in Energy Cooperation', *The World Today*, **34** (March 1978).

Tussie, Diana, 'Latin American Integration: from LAFTA to LAIA', *Journal of World Trade Law*, **16** (1982), 399–413.

Twitchett, Carol Cosgrove, 'Towards a New ACP-EC Convention', *The World Today*, **34** (December 1978).

Twomey, Michael J., 'Economic Fluctuations in Argentina, Australia, and Canada during the Depression of the 1930s' (unpublished paper presented to the International Congress of Americanists, Manchester, UK, September 1982).

United Nations Conference on Trade and Development, *Towards a New Trade Policy for Development: report by the Secretary-General of the United Nations Conference on Trade and Development* (New York, United Nations, 1964).

United Nations Department of Political and Security Council Affairs, *The United Nations and Disarmament, 1970–75* (New York, United Nations, 1975).

Vernon, Raymond, *Storm over the Multinationals: the Real Issues* (London, Macmillan, 1977).

Walters, R. S., 'International Organization and Political Communications: the Use of UNCTAD by Less Developed Countries', *International Organization*, **25** (1971), 818–35.

Ward, Barbara, 'Another Chance for the North?', *Foreign Affairs*, **59** (1980/81), 386–97.

Wassermann, Ursula, 'The Common Fund', *Journal of World Trade Law*, **11** (1977), 377–9.

Wassermann, Ursula, 'WIPO: the Exclusion of South Africa?', *Journal of World Trade Law*, **14** (1980), 78–80.

Wassermann, Ursula, 'WIPO: Diplomatic Patent Conference', *Journal of World Trade Law*, **14** (1980), 254–6.

Wassermann, Ursula, 'Law of the Sea Convention Adopted', *Journal of World Trade Law*, **16** (1982), 440–4.

Weintraub, Sidney, 'The New International Economic Order: the Beneficiaries', *World Development*, **7** (1979), 247–58.

Weintraub, Sidney, 'What Life is Left in the North–South Dialogue?', *The World Economy*, **2** (1980), 453–65.

West, Rebecca, *Black Lamb and Grey Falcon: the record of a journey through Yugoslavia in 1937* (London, Macmillan, 1942).

White, John, 'The New International Economic Order: what is it?', *International Affairs*, **54** (1978), 626–34.

Wijkman, Magnus Per, 'UNCLOS and the Redistribution of Ocean Wealth', *Journal of World Trade Law*, **16** (1982), 27–48.

Willetts, Peter, *The Non-Aligned in Havana* (London, Frances Pinter, 1981).

Williams, Maurice J., 'The Aid Problems of OPEC Countries', *Foreign Affairs*, **54** (1976), 308–24.

Woodrow Wilson Study Group (William Y. Elliott, chairman), *The Political Economy of American Foreign Policy: Its Concepts, Strategy, and Limits* (New York, Henry Holt, 1955).

Young, Simon Z., *Terms of Entry* (London, Heinemann, 1973), pp. 154–66.

Younger, Sam, 'Ideology and Pragmatism in Algerian Foreign Policy', *The World Today*, 34 (March 1978), 112-14.

Zammit, Ann, 'UNCTAD III: End of an Illusion', *IDS Bulletin*, 5 (1973).

Zorn, Stephen A., 'Producers' Associations and Commodity Markets: the Case of CIPEC', in F. Gerard Adams and Sonia A. Klein, eds, *Stabilizing World Commodity Markets* (Lexington, Mass., Lexington Books, 1978).

INDEX